TRAVELLERS

ONTARIO &
QUÉBEC

By
STEVE VEALE

Written by Steve Veale

Original photography by Donald Nausbaum

Editing and page layout by Cambridge Publishing Management Ltd,
Unit 2, Burr Elm Court, Caldecote CB23 7NU
Series Editor: Karen Beaulah

Published by Thomas Cook Publishing
A division of Thomas Cook Tour Operations Ltd
Company Registration No. 1450464 England

PO Box 227, The Thomas Cook Business Park,
Coningsby Road, Peterborough PE3 8SB, United Kingdom
E-mail: books@thomascook.com
www.thomascookpublishing.com
Tel: +44 (0)1733 416477

ISBN: 978-1-84157-827-9

Text © 2007 Thomas Cook Publishing
Maps © 2007 Thomas Cook Publishing
Toronto transport map © 2007 Communicarta Ltd

Project Editor: Rebecca Snelling
Production/DTP Editor: Steven Collins

Printed and bound in Italy by: Printer Trento.

Front cover credits L–R: © Ralph A. Clevenger/Corbis,
© Paul A. Souders/Corbis, © Wolfgang Kaehler/Corbis
Back cover credits L–R: © Andreas Achmann/4 Corners Images,
© Ralf Krahmer/4 Corners Images

Contents

Introduction

The story of Canada's tourism is best described as 'Moose, Mountains and Mounties'. People think of Canada as a country of untamed wilderness, endless forests, countless rivers and streams, miles and miles (or kilometres and kilometres) of uncharted territory. And while all that is true, visitors will also find urban delights in some of the great cities of North America such as Toronto and Montreal, Ottawa and Québec City.

Ontario and Québec best define the often schizophrenic nature of the country as French and English share an invisible border; it's as if the English Channel disappeared overnight and come next morning, England and France discovered that they were jammed together. Or to quote the title of Canadian author Hugh Maclennan's well-known novel, Ontario and Québec are indeed *Two Solitudes*.

That is not to say they aren't friendly and show respect for each other, but one is definitely Anglophile, while the other is decidedly Francophone. And as the French say '*Vive la différence*'!

Ontario and Québec can lay claim to the two largest urban centres in the country, and therefore the two largest centres for business, commerce, communications, arts and leisure. A bonus for both provinces is that the

The city of Montréal at night

Nation's Capital in the Ottawa-Gatineau region spans the borders between them – connected by bridges across the Ottawa River.

The four major cities of each province – Toronto and Ottawa, Montreal and Québec – are filled with 21st-century urban wonders that are home to the performing arts of dance, music and every type of eclectic entertainment one can imagine in a 'big city' environment (the now world famous Cirque de Soleil started life on the streets of Québec City). There are art and sculpture galleries galore, and museums filled with scientific marvels, dinosaur bones and Elton John's shoes (!). You will find trendy accommodation with chic, five-star grandeur and cosy little inexpensive B&Bs, and restaurants, cafés and pubs that include some of the world's finest dining.

But outside those main cities is another world entirely – a world of untamed wilderness, with millions of watery kilometers that connect a seemingly unlimited number of lakes and rivers. Sports and recreational activities include mountain biking, skiing and hiking; there are campsites of incredible solitude where the only sounds are the loons at night and perhaps a wolf call in the distant forest. The fun and frivolity of sailing, waterskiing and golf can be found at some of the world's best luxury resorts.

A visitor to Ontario and Québec should allow enough time to experience the incredible duality of each province – not just English and French, but discoveries found along city streets and country trails.

A Canadian Mountie

Introduction

The land

In historical terms, Canada is still a very, very young nation. Officially it only became a country on 1 July 1867. However, the founding history goes back much further than that.

The Canada of present day is the second-largest country in the world (after Russia) with an estimated 9,976,139sq km (3,850,789sq miles) of land.

There are six natural geographical regions that stretch coast-to-coast across this massive area. They are: the Appalachian Region, the Great Lakes-St Lawrence Lowlands, the Canadian Shield, the Interior Plains, the Western Cordilleras and the Arctic Islands.

The combined landmass of Ontario and Québec is an astounding 2,426,582sq km (936,909sq miles); Québec is the largest at 1,358sq km (524,300sq miles) and Ontario is second biggest at 1,068,582sq km (412,580sq miles).

Ontario's name is derived from either the Iroquois or Huron dialect meaning 'beautiful or sparkling water', due to the province's more than half-a-million lakes. Northern Ontario also has a saltwater shoreline of 1,210km (752 miles). This proximity to water, combined with the moderating influence of weather around the Niagara Escarpment has created excellent farming communities and a thriving wine industry.

The native Algonquin tribe of Québec named the first settlement 'Kebec' ('where the river narrows') and the name stuck for both the city and the province. About 80% of the province is situated within the rocky Canadian Shield and is filled with lakes and rivers big and small, impenetrable forests and rolling plateaux.

The first inhabitants of these two provinces were the native Indian, Inuit and Eskimo tribes, and attempts to colonise the land commenced following the voyages of Christopher Columbus to 'The New World'. The first recognised discovery was recorded on 24 June 1497 by John Cabot who reached the shores of Newfoundland and claimed the land for England. Then in 1534, French explorer Jacques Cartier landed on the shores of Gaspé and claimed the land for France.

The French established themselves in an area between Montréal and Québec City known as 'Lower Canada', while the English controlled the area to the southwest, then called 'Upper Canada'.

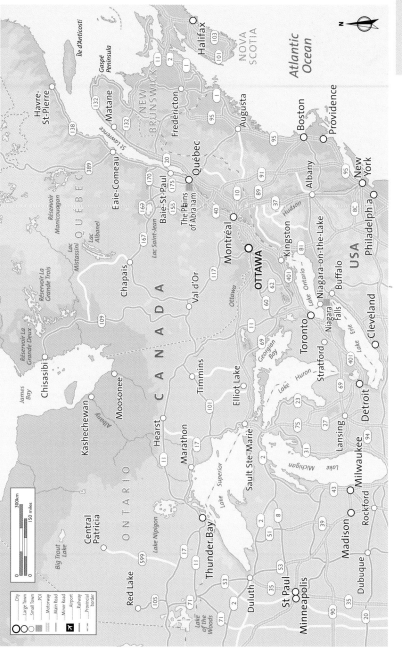

History

1497 Canada is officially discovered when John Cabot lands on Newfoundland.

1504 St John's Newfoundland becomes the first established settlement in North America.

1535 French explorer Jacques Cartier discovers the St Lawrence River. He climbs to the top of a nearby mountain which he names 'Mont Real'. Cartier gives Canada its name when he mistakes the Indian word Kannata ('a collection of huts') for the name of the entire country.

1608 Québec City is founded by Samuel de Champlain – explorer, cartographer, writer.

1610–11 English navigator Henry Hudson discovers Hudson's Bay while seeking the elusive Northwest Passage to the East.

1759 The Battle of Québec takes place on the Plains of Abraham as the British defeat the French in a bid to establish control of Canada.

1763 The defeat becomes official at the Treaty of Paris in 1763 when the French surrender all its possessions in North America, except for the fishing rights on the little islands of St Pierre and Miquelon.

1792 The First Legislature of Upper Canada opens at Newark (now Niagara-on-the-Lake).

1792 The First Legislature of Lower Canada opens in Québec City.

1812 The colonies in the United States declare war on Britain and therefore on Canada.

1829 Welland Canal opens, providing a passageway between Lake Erie and Lake Ontario for ship transportation through the Great Lakes.

1837 Rebellions in Lower Canada, led by Louis Joseph Papineau, and in Upper Canada by William Lyon Mackenzie to protest the dictatorial powers of the government. The rebellions are crushed; 12 rebels are hanged and others sent to penal colonies.

1847 Alexander Graham Bell invents the telephone and places the world's first long-distance call between Brantford and Paris (Ontario).

1857 Queen Victoria settles various rival claims to 'the Capital of Canada' by choosing Ottawa as the official capital.

1867 The British North American Act establishes Canada's Confederation on 1 July 1867 when statesmen from the various colonies officially declare this 'The Dominion of Canada'.

1884 First votes for women in Ontario municipal elections; the ballots, however, are given only to widows and spinsters.

1914 Canada enters World War I.

1939 Canada enters World War II.

1953 Canada's National Library is established in Ottawa.

1953 The world-famous Stratford Festival, in Stratford, Ontario, opens on a wooden stage under a tent.

1959 The St Lawrence Seaway is officially opened at the St Lambert Lock in Montréal by Queen Elizabeth II and US President Dwight Eisenhower.

1967 The country celebrates 100 years of confederation (1 July) with the massive Expo '67 in Montréal.

1974 National Assembly of Québec adopts French as the only official language of Québec (although the federal government has adopted a bilingual policy).

1976 Montréal hosts the Olympic Summer Games.

1982 Canadian Prime Minister Pierre Elliott Trudeau and the Liberal government gain a new Constitution and Charter of Rights and Freedom for the country, effectively repatriating the BNA Act of 1867.

1984 Trudeau resigns and elections are won by the Progressive Conservatives led by Brian Mulroney.

1993 Mulroney is succeeded by Kim Campbell, Canada's first female Prime Minister.

1995 A referendum on independence in Québec is rejected by just 1%.

2006 Conservatives win the general election, bringing an end to 12 years of Liberal rule.

Politics

Canada is a democratic country with a federal system of government (and legal matters) based on the British system. The Canadian parliament, or the House of Commons, is located in the nation's Capital Region of Ottawa, Ontario and just across the Ottawa River in Gatineau, Québec.

There are three elements that make up the federal government; the Queen (represented by the governor general), the Senate (a total of 105 members chosen by the prime minister) and the House of Commons, which controls the day-to-day political agenda of the elected politicians.

There are a total of 308 representatives democratically elected from the 12 provinces of Canada. Politicians are elected in a free vote every four or five years. (Though a majority government has the possibility of a five-year mandate, the prime minister is free to call on the governor general to dissolve parliament and declare an election at any time during his or her term.)

The major parties in the federal government are the Progressive Conservatives (Tories), the Liberals, the New Democratic Party and the Bloc Québecois. (Though it is considered a national political party, the Bloc is solely Québec-based; its founding principle is to separate from Canada and gain 'sovereignty' for Québec.) *Federal and provincial government information. www.parl.gc.ca*

Ontario

The Legislative Building at Queen's Park (the site really is a park), known informally as 'The Ledge', is where Ontario's elected Members of Provincial Parliament (MPPs) make the decisions that shape Ontario's future. Aside from the formal chamber, many of the MPPs have their offices in this building.

The Chamber is an imposing room, in keeping with its important role in the democratic system. Massive panels of intricately carved mahogany and sycamore deck the four-storey walls right up to a magnificent ceiling fresco – hidden since 1912 by a layer of acoustic tiles.

The person who occupies that chair is the speaker. The speaker is chief presiding officer of the House, with final authority on all matters of order and procedure.

There are a total of 103 elected MPPs in the Legislature (two-thirds of whom are Liberals, followed by the Conservatives and the New Democratic Party). The premier of the province is Dalton McGuinty, leader of the Liberal Party.

Public tours of the Ontario Legislature are available during the week.
Queen's Park, Toronto ON M7A 1A1. Tel: (416) 326-1234. www.gov.on.ca

Québec

The National Assembly of Québec is composed of 125 members elected by the population in each electoral division under the single member constituency system. The Assembly and the lieutenant-governor form the parliament of Québec. Under this British-style parliamentary system, the parliament and the government represent two distinct levels of power: legislative and executive.

The premier and the ministers, together with the lieutenant-governor, exercise executive power. Legislative power resides in the parliament. Members are responsible for overseeing the actions of the government and government departments and bodies, and serve as mediators between electors of their constituency and the public administration.

Led by Premier Jean Charest, the Liberal Party forms the government, holding over half the seats, the

House of Commons in Ottawa

separatist Partis Québecois holds about a third, with a few held by the Action democratique du Québec.

The building itself was designed by architect Eugène-Étienne Taché and built between 1877 and 1886 on Québec's foremost national historic site. Inspired by the Louvre, the building most representative of Second Empire-style architecture, Taché's imposing work is unique in North America. Guided tours are offered throughout the week, and admission is free.

Though Canada is officially a bilingual country, the National Assembly passed a law in 1977 making French the only official language in Québec.
Parlement Building, 1045 rue des Parlementaires, Québec G1A 1A3. Tel: (418) 643-7239. www.assnat.qc.ca

VIA Rail

Canada is a country forged and connected by commercial, industrial and passenger rail transportation – the Western Provinces and British Columbia agreed to join in the proposed Confederation of Canada only if there was a coast-to-coast rail line uniting every province. (For the complete picture, read Pierre Berton's book *The Last Spike* or listen to Canadian troubadour Gordon Lightfoot's musical homage *Great Railroad Trilogy*.) Even these days, when one can zoom from coast to coast in a few hours by jet, the three-day cross-Canada VIA Rail passenger cars are still amazingly popular, and always filled with both Canadians

Rail track through Canadian mountains

and visitors who want to see this massive country and its changing landscape from the comfort of their window seats.

The two original rail companies, Canadian National (CN) and Canadian Pacific (CP), now transport only goods and merchandise, while VIA Rail Canada is responsible for all passenger services.

VIA Rail

VIA Rail, an independent Crown corporation established in 1978, operates trains in all regions of Canada over an east–west rail network from the Atlantic Coast to the Pacific and north from the Great Lakes to Hudson Bay. In statistical terms, VIA trains run over 14,000km (8,700 miles) of track, serving some 450 Canadian communities.

And they are busy. Very busy. VIA transports 3.9 million passengers every year. The company employs a staff of more than 3,000 on some 480 trains per week.

Popular routes

The busiest route in the country is the well-travelled corridor between Windsor and Québec City. In fact,

VIA train carriage

during autumn 2006, VIA Rail commemorated the 150th anniversary of the first passenger train between Toronto and Montréal. That journey, on 26 October 1856, was made in a record time of 14 hours. The track was soon extended to stretch from the Detroit US border crossing at Windsor to Québec City in the east.

The 1,150-km (715-mile) Windsor–Québec City Corridor in Central Canada winds through the most densely populated and heavily industrialised area of the country. This region contains over half of Canada's population – 16 million – and some of its largest cities.

Every week, more than 400 of Canada's intercity passenger trains (with assigned seating) run between the major cities in the corridor, and every railway station is located in the heart of each major city – Windsor, Toronto, Ottawa, Montréal and Québec City. There is no need to worry about getting into traffic jams en route to the airport, arriving two hours pre-flight or worrying about delays due to weather conditions.

Outdoor facilities

There are two available classes – Comfort (Economy), and VIA, which features more space, a delicious meal and first-class check-in at the station's Panorama lounge. And on the train, VIA 1 passenger tickets also enjoy exclusive access to the VIA 1 lounge.

Since the Windsor–Québec City Corridor is an important route for business travellers as well as a plethora of university students, VIA introduced wireless Internet access on board every train travelling along this corridor – the first passenger rail operator in North America to provide this complimentary service.
Tel: (514) 871-6000. Toll-free in Canada (888) VIA-RAIL ((888) 842-7245). www.viarail.ca

Culture

Cultural events, fall fairs, festivals and sporting events are held throughout Ontario – from the Binder Twine Festival in Kleinburg to Winterlude in Ottawa, the Friendship Festival in Simcoe to Oktoberfest in Kitchener-Waterloo, Fish Fest in Port Dover to the Native Pow Wow on Manitoulin Island. Québec has a proud and historic background of French culture and customs dating back to the founding of Québec City almost 400 years ago.

Ontario

You can find a community fair or festival every weekend of the year in Ontario. However, there is no other city in the world that has as many combined cultures, customs, societies and religions as Toronto; at the last count there were more than 100 languages and countries from around the world represented in the multicultural fabric of this city. Toronto holds annual festivals and events that highlight these cultures and lifestyles.

Totem Pole at the Royal Ontario Museum

Some cultural statistics:

- Toronto is home to more than 200 professional theatre and dance companies.
- The city is the third-largest English-speaking language theatre centre in the world.
- There are more art schools in Toronto than any other North American city.
- Known as 'Hollywood North', there can be up to 40 productions (including feature films and TV series) filming in Toronto at any given time.
- There are 7,000 heritage properties in the city including well-known cultural and historic structures.
- Toronto has 125 museums ranging from the massive Royal Ontario Museum to the hands-on Stock Market Place.

Some of the cultural highlights include the following:

Toronto International Film Festival
See pp34–5.

Caribana
The largest celebration of Caribbean culture in North America takes place every July as the city morphs into island fever with an infectious reggae/calypso beat. The final festival is held on the first weekend in August on the Toronto Island.

Pride Week
What started as a little Sunday-afternoon parade in June along Church Street has burgeoned into a celebration of gay and lesbian lifestyles attracting at least one million people to the city.

Québec
Montréal presents 90 festivals, including the annual world-renowned Montréal Jazz Festival and Just for Laughs extravaganza, every year. There are more than 200 professional theatre companies in Montréal, some 50 dance companies, two symphony orchestras and at least a dozen contemporary music ensembles.

With an average of some 21 shows per evening, even the most dedicated lover of theatre, concerts, music and entertainment cannot keep up with this explosion of arts. Of course, being a francophone city, many of these theatrical performances are in French; it will be easy to determine just by reading (or not!) the language of the advertisement. Dance and music are more of a universal language.

Cinémathèque québécoise
The Cinémathèque québécoise is Montréal's museum of the moving image. Every year, there are more than 1,500 screenings of films, television programmes and videos from all eras and countries, with free access to the exhibitions. The Guy-L-Côté Mediatheque is one of the most important cinema documentation centres in America (guided tours for school groups).
335 de Maisonneuve Boulevard East.
Tel: (514) 842-9763.
www.cinematheque.qc.ca

Centaur Theatre
Centaur is Québec's premier English-language theatre company. Founded in 1969 by Maurice Podbrey and Herbert C Auerbach, and based in the former Montréal Stock Exchange, Centaur has two theatres and presents a six-play line-up ranging from contemporary Canadian dramas to Broadway hits.
453 rue Saint-François-Xavier.
Tel: (514) 288-3161.
www.centaurtheatre.com

Le Festin du Gouverneur
Since 1973 the Festin du Gouverneur has put on dinner-shows in English and French, featuring artists, troubadours in period costume, operatic numbers, and Québec and Irish ballads.
Old Fort at Île Sainte-Hélène.
Tel: (514) 879-1141.
www.festin.com

Festivals and events

Ontario and Québec have numerous events that are well worth a visit if they coincide with your trip, including fairs and carnivals in both summer and winter.

Toronto

Canadian National Exhibition (Toronto)

One of the city's most beloved traditions since 1879, the CNE is the largest fair in Canada, complete with rides, games of chance, musical entertainment, animals and games for the children, greasy junk food from the hundreds of fast-food stands and a never-ending supply of more up-market culinary samples and new food products from the ever-popular Food Building. The roots of this annual three-week fair and exhibition can still be found in the buildings featuring prize-winning apple pies and huge pumpkins as well as the horse shows and petting zoos for the children. *Lakeshore Boulevard West. Tel: (416) 263-3800. www.TheEx.com*

Royal Agricultural Winter Fair (Toronto)

If it is November in Toronto, it is time for 'The Royal' – two weeks of all things agricultural, horticultural, canine and equestrian. This is the largest such event in the world and an excellent opportunity for 'city kids' to appreciate the lives of their country cousins in the vast rural areas of the province. There is also a very smart horse show that always captures the élite of Toronto society. *Exhibition Place (CNE grounds). Tel: (416) 263-3400. www.royalfair.org*

Québec

Québec Winter Carnival

When the white mantle of winter drapes itself on Québec, it's Carnival time! Tradition says that Samuel de Champlain started this event almost 400 years ago in an attempt to maintain the cheerful spirits of his men during the coldest month of the year.

This carnival celebrates winter with snow sculptures, night parades, slide runs, a giant table-soccer game, musical concerts, sleigh rides, dogsled runs, and any silly activity that will take your mind off the minus 40°C (minus 40°F) weather from the end of January to mid-February.

The modern version of this historic event will mark it 54th edition during the 2008 celebrations of the city's 400th anniversary. The theme will include athletic competitions, spectacular skiing and skating demonstrations, and many, many winter games for carnival-goers. *Tel: 1-866-4-Carnaval (422-7628). www.carnaval.qc.ca*

Hôtel de Glace Québec-Canada

Québec's Ice Hotel is an amazing 3,000sq m (3,588sq yd) complex made entirely of snow and ice. Located inside you will find the popular ABSOLUT ice bar, ice chapel, two exhibition rooms, 34 rooms and theme suites (one special suite has a fireplace), and a huge N'Ice Club with a capacity of 400 people. There are also two outdoor hot tubs and a sauna. Enjoy a full array of winter activities, including dog sledding and ice fishing (equipment rentals offered on site). Located at the Station Touristique Duchesnay (25 minutes west of Québec City).

Pavillon La Régie, 14 route Duchesnay, Sainte-Catherine-de-la-Jacques-Cartie. Tel: (418) 875-45221 or (877) 505-0423.

Cirque du Soleil

From humble beginnings on the cobblestone streets of Vieux-Québec, this 'circus without animals' has become one of the true wonders of international entertainment. There are now several troupes around the world

(including a permanent home in Las Vegas) performing impossible contortionist feats to the astonishment of every audience. The cirque unveils its new acts every year during the spring. *Tel: (800) 361-4595. www.cirquedusoleil.com*

Québec City Summer Festival (Vieux-Québec)

As a counterpoint to its chilly activities in the winter, the residents of Québec hold a summer festival every July throughout the Old City. The cobblestone streets are not only filled with tourists but clowns and jugglers, musicians and singers, entertainers and artists too.

Tel: (418) 523-4540 or (888) 992-5200. www.infofestival.com

Entrance to Hôtel de Glace Québec-Canada

Highlights

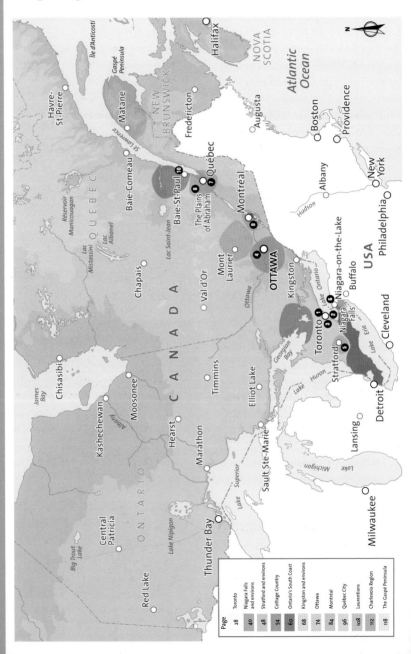

Ontario

① CN Tower (Toronto) Although it may be a cliché for residents of Canada's biggest city, the CN Tower is still the most popular – and recognisable – symbol of Toronto. Day or night, it is undeniably one of the most beautiful urban panoramas in the world. A view from the observation deck will help the visitor put Toronto into perspective; the neighbourhoods, the parks, the easy grid system of streets and avenues as well as the southern view of the harbourfront and Toronto Islands are all clearly laid out for you far below your feet. It is always a thrill to book a table in the Tower's 360 Restaurant and take a couple of revolutions around Toronto during your meal.
301 Front Street West. Tel: (416) 360-8500. www.cntower.ca

② The Toronto Islands Nowhere is the lushness of Toronto's greenery more evident than on the Toronto Islands; it is the perfect spot for strollers, cyclists, swimmers and sun-worshippers, just a five-minute ferry ride from the harbour.
See Walk, pp38–9.

③ Toronto streetcars Toronto is one of two cities in North America (San Francisco being the other) that still has working trolley cars along its busy downtown streets. Though residents may take them

for granted, any suggestion to discontinue the service is always met with vigorous and vocal opposition.

The subway may be faster, but this is the best way to view the city and all its neighbourhoods; for example, the No 504 along Dundas Street will transport riders through Chinatown, Portugal and Italy within five streetcar stops. A one-day TTC (Toronto Transit Commission) pass will provide unlimited access to interconnecting streetcars, subways and bus routes.
Toronto Transit Commission. www.ttc.ca

④ Parliament Hill (Ottawa) The home of the federal government of Canada, built between 1859 and 1866, consists of stunning neo-Gothic buildings of granite, stone and copper. The parliament buildings command an impressive view of the Ottawa River. Guests may also sit in the Visitors' Gallery in the House of Commons if they wish to hear the yammering of politicians.
(See also Ottawa, p74.)
Wellington Street. Tel: (613) 996-0896. www.parl.gc.ca

⑤ Hiking The Stratford Festival (City of Stratford) Formerly a small farming community, this rural town is filled with trendy

shops and chic boutiques, fine dining, up-market accommodation, fancy B&Bs, art galleries, cafés and pubs – all due to a wooden stage under a tent that transformed a sleepy rural community into one of the major theatre centres in the world. (*See also pp52–3.*)
City of Stratford. Box 818. Stratford. Tel: (800) 561-SWA, or (519) 271-5140. www.city.stratford.on.ca Stratford Festival. Stratford. Tel: (800) 567-1600 or (519) 271-4040. www.stratfordfestival.ca

❻ The Shaw Festival (Niagara-on-the-Lake) At first glance, the main street of this little community seems frozen in a mid-18th-century time warp; the boutiques are filled with homemade jams and jellies, Irish linens and Scottish tweeds. The accommodation and restaurants, however, are strictly first-class 21st century. Like its counterpart in Stratford-upon-Avon, the Shaw Festival turned this tiny village into a tourist haven and 'must-see' for international theatre-lovers. (*See also p47.*)
Niagara-on-the-Lake Chamber of Commerce/VCB. 153 King Street. Tel: (905) 468-1950. www.niagaraonthelake.com The Shaw Festival. 10 Queen's Parade. Tel: (800) 657-110 or (905) 468-2153. www.shawfest.com

Québec

❼ Vieux-Québec This living museum of 16th-century French architecture, houses and churches has become one of the most thriving, colourful and fun areas not only of Québec but of the entire country. The walled city – one of the few such UNESCO World Heritage Sites – is packed with both locals and visitors who relax in fine French restaurants, pavement cafés, old pubs and dozens of art galleries in old stone-and-mortar houses that were built four centuries ago. (*See also p97.*)
Québec City. www.quebecregion.com

❽ The Plains of Abraham & battlements (National Historic Sites) This parkland is arguably the most historic site in Canada because a short-lived battle in 1759 determined the fate and future of this country; the ongoing battle for control of the New World was sealed when the British army scaled the cliffs of the St Lawrence in a surprise attack on the French army.

Today this huge urban 45-ha (110-acre) park is always filled with strollers, bikers and many enjoying a picnic lunch on the sloping green hills looking down on the waters of the St Lawrence. Visitors, especially history buffs, should also explore the nearby fortifications, Citadelle and Artillery Park.
Battlefields Park. Tel: (418) 648-

4071. Email:
information@ccbn-nbc.gc.ca

Tel: (514) 496-7678.
www.oldportofmontreal.com

9 **Vieux Montréal & Old Port** Very
few cities in North America have a
romantic, historic and French-
tinged district filled with 17th-
century buildings, cobblestone
streets and horse-drawn carriages.
As you stroll around the old
streets, you soon start to relax in a
bygone era of 400-year-old
buildings now filled with
restaurants, art galleries and
boutiques. Take a ride at night in a
calèche along rue Sainte-Hélène, lit
by gas street lamps, and you will
swear you are in 17th-century
Paris. The adjoining Old Port
district is a stretch of history that
is now a tourist haven filled with
cafés and activities all along the
old harbourfront.
Old Port. Rue de la Commune.

10 **Baie-St-Paul (Charlevoix)** For
those who wish to experience the
charm of a small Québec village,
Baie-St-Paul is a one-hour drive
from Québec City, in the beautiful
artists' enclave of Charlevoix. The
village on the bay is one of the
oldest and most charming places
in Québec. Today the centuries-old
main street is rife with art galleries,
craft boutiques, cosy cafés,
welcoming B&Bs and – of course –
hearty homemade French rural
cooking. This is truly a picture-
postcard village that combines the
charms of an historic community
with the amenities of this century.
You can catch a ferry from the
harbour to the nearby Île-aux-
Coudres (*see p114*).
www.tourisme-charlevois.com

Artillery Park, The Plains of Abraham

Ontario spas

Though there have always been a few spas in the province, the industry blossomed at the turn of the 21st century. Some new first-class spa facilities (many connected with country resorts) appeared throughout the province while the existing ones underwent major renovation to greet a 'spa-hungry' public. With this sudden interest in spas from residents and visitors alike, the industry created Premier Spas of Ontario: a self-regulating body that assures clients of the highest quality of services and treatments in selected establishments across the province.

Entrance to Hockley Valley Resort

In a former incarnation, spas were seen as little more than up-market beauty salons for privileged society matrons who might go for an afternoon session of facials and pedicures. Ontario has both challenged and changed that concept, and made it acceptable for anyone to turn to spa therapy to conquer stress, whether old or young, male or female.

The mandate for the Ontario spa industry is to promote health and wellbeing, which is also a cornerstone of the official policy statement issued by the provincial government.

At present there are less than 30 spas across the province that have passed the rigorous qualifications and been accepted into the Premier Spas of Ontario listings. These facilities have passed the highest scrutiny and the public can feel assured they are receiving the best treatment from a certified professional; the spa itself must meet quality standards from a list of more than 80 requirements.

In fact, to even apply for membership, an establishment must offer a minimum of three types of massage treatment (e.g. Swedish massage, shiatsu), two treatments of alternative massage (e.g. stone

Enjoy being pampered at an Ontario spa resort

massage or wraps) three body treatments (e.g. reflexology and reiki) and at least four skin care services (e.g. glycolac peels and collagen treatments).

Many of the spas are located in the populated corridor region stretching from Toronto to Niagara. However, they are also scattered throughout Ontario, in quieter rural settings such as Gravenhurst, Zephyr, Picton and Honey Harbour, very often as part of a large five-star resort or rustic hidden-away country inn.

Premier Spas of Ontario. Spas Ontario, 176 Napier Street, Barrie, Ontario L4M 1W8. Tel: (705) 721-9969 or (800) 990-7702. Email: info@premierspasofontario.ca. www.premierspasofontario.ca.

The following is a selection of Premier Spas located throughout the province.

Deerhurst Resort *Huntsville. Tel: (705) 789-6411. www.deerhurstresort.com*

Elmwood Spa *18 Elm Street, Toronto. Tel: (416) 977-6751. www.elmwoodspa.com*

Healthwinds Spa *2401 Yonge Street, Toronto. Tel: (416) 488-9545. www.healthwindsspa.com*

Hockley Valley Resort *R.R. 1 Orangeville. Tel: (416) 363-5490. www.hockley.com*

The Inn at Manitou *McKellar, Ontario. Tel: (705) 389-2171. www.manitou-online.com*

Langdon Hall Country House Hotel With brand-new 21st-century spa facilities. *Cambridge, Ontario. Tel: (519) 740-2100. www.langdonhall.com*

Millcroft Inn *Alton, Ontario. Tel: (519) 941-8111. www.millcroft.com*

ScapeSpa *Mount Pleasant, Ontario. Tel: (519) 484-1110. www.scapespa.com*

Secret Garden Spa Located in the luxurious 114-room *Prince of Wales Hotel. 6 Picton Street, Niagara-on-the-Lake. Tel: (905) 468-3246. www.vintageinns.com*

The Spa at White Oaks Conference Resort. *253 Taylor Road, Niagara-on-the-Lake. Tel: (905) 688-2032. www.whiteoaksresort.com*

Suggested itineraries

Visitors who are driving through Ontario and Québec have the choice of zooming along a superhighway that will connect them to all the major cities en route or dawdling along country roads and exploring the vast rural areas of the two provinces.

First-time visitors are always amazed at the sheer size of these two provinces and often don't realise how much time it takes to travel between major sites and cities. For instance, those entering by car at the Detroit-Windsor border can simply stay on Highway 401 that will take them through London, Hamilton, Toronto, Kingston, Cornwall and right to the Québec border. At that point the name changes to Highway 20 into Montréal and then Highway 40 follows the St Lawrence Seaway right into Québec City – a distance of approximately 1,100km (684 miles).

Long weekend

For those with just a limited amount of time – say, four days – and who wish to experience both provinces on a whirlwind tour, take the drive between Toronto (*see p28*) and Montréal (*see p84*), or vice versa. This is about six hours (see route above) with a couple of quick coffee stops along the highway. This will only give you a day or two in each city, but will let you experience the cultural difference between Anglo Toronto's CN Tower (*see p29*) and Francophone Montréal's Mont Royal (*see p91*). A more relaxed option, depending on your starting point, would be a combination of Toronto and Ottawa (*see p74*) or Montréal and Ottawa.

One week

A much more comprehensive road trip would stretch from Toronto to Ottawa, then across the border to Montréal and Québec City. Not only will you be able to enjoy the 'big cities', but also relax on the rural highways and byways of eastern Ontario (Kingston, *see p68*, and Prince Edward County, *see p73*) and southern Québec. This trip should include at least one overnight stay in the Nation's Capital, and a more relaxed drive between Montréal and Québec City, which will allow you to visit such diverse cultural icons as the Shrine of Sainte-Anne-de-Beaupré (*see p103*) as well as the many famous 'chip wagons' (*see p116*) in the Québec countryside.

Two weeks

This is the perfect length for a two-province visit – it allows you to spend more time in each of the major cities listed above, but also add on Québec's artistic and culinary Charlevoix region (*see p112*) as well as Niagara Falls (*see p40*), Niagara-on-the-Lake (*see p46*) and Stratford (*see p48*) in Ontario. Avoid summer weekends if you are planning to

The Canadian parliament building in Ottawa

Driving through Ontario in the autumn

visit the Falls – it is incredibly crowded. And make sure you book tickets and accommodation well in advance for any visit to the Stratford or Shaw Festivals (*see pp52–3 & 47*). Make sure you have time to visit the Mennonite areas of St Jacobs and Elora, too (*see pp50–51*).

Longer visits

Those who have the luxury of time and a sense of exploration should leave the populated areas of each province behind and head into the hinterlands of Québec, such as the Gaspé Peninsula (*see p118*) along the south shore of the province. You could also drive through the brilliant autumn leaves of the Laurentians (*see p108*) or maybe even fly out to the tiny Îles de la Madeleine (*see p124*) in the Gulf of St Lawrence. Those

who wish to see Ontario's northern towns and villages can travel along a ribbon of roads stretching some 2,000km (1,243 miles) from Toronto to the Manitoba border.

Along the way you'll get to ride on the Chi Cheemaun ferry across to Manitoulin Island (*see p66*), explore the mining town of Sudbury (*see p128*), watch the huge lock systems at U.S. border crossing of Sault Ste Marie (*see p128*), chug into the impenetrable wilderness on the Agawa Canyon Railway (*see p129*) and view the magnificent cliff of the Ouiment Canyon Provincial Park just outside of Thunder Bay, and finally stay in a little cosy cabin on one of the many quiet bays of Kenora's Lake of the Woods (*see p131*).

Québec's Old Port

Toronto

Located approximately in the middle of the country, Toronto is the largest city in Canada, the financial centre of the nation and the capital for the provincial government of Ontario. The population of Greater Toronto is approximately 4.7 million people, the fifth-largest city on the North American continent (after Mexico City, New York, Los Angeles and Chicago).

Sounds massive, doesn't it? Not really. Although this is a busy city, the centre of government and commerce, it is also a relaxed, friendly and above all safe urban playground filled with green parkland and international neighbourhoods such as Chinese and Portuguese lying cheek by jowl.

Tourism Toronto. Queen's Quay Terminal at Harbourfront. 207 Queen's Quay West. Tel: (416) 203-2600.
www.torontotourism.com

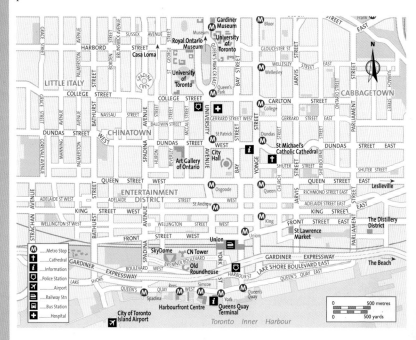

CENTRAL TORONTO
Art Gallery of Ontario (AGO)

Like its counterparts the Royal Ontario Museum (ROM) and Gardiner Museum, the AGO has also just emerged from a multi-million-dollar renovation and expansion. The design, by famed architect Frank Gehry, was created in part to hold the works donated by the late media mogul Ken Thomson who bequeathed his sizeable art collection to the AGO. The gallery is a spacious, well-designed and approachable building that seems to encourage the visitor to wander among the galleries of history and style – ranging from Canada's Group of Seven (*see p35*) and Henry Moore to works by Chagall and Picasso.

317 Dundas Street West. Tel: (416) 979-6648. www.ago.net. Open: Tue–Sun 10am–8pm. Closed: Mon. Admission charge.

Casa Loma

A little bit of Europe in Toronto. This 'castle-on-a-hill' was commissioned in 1907 by local magnate Sir Henry Pellatt as a gift to his young bride. Architect E J Lennox finished the medieval-style 98-room castle in 1914, complete with gargoyles, corbelled towers and battlements, 21 fireplaces and secret passageways; something you would find looming out of the mists of the Scottish moors.

1 Austin Terrace. Tel: (416) 923-1171. www.casaloma.org. Open: daily 9.30am–5pm. Admission charge.

CN Tower

Look up – way, way up. At 553m (1,815ft) the CN Tower is still the world's tallest structure. Though originally built in 1976 as the city's cornerstone for communications – the world's tallest television antennae – the structure itself has become synonymous with the city and one of its most popular attractions. To avoid the crowded elevators, book a table at the 360 Restaurant. There is a separate elevator for dining visitors and you can enjoy the complete 360-degree view in relaxed, jostle-free luxury.

301 Front Street West. Tel: (416) 360-8500. www.cntower.ca. Open: daily 9am–10pm. Admission charge.

The Distillery District

This is a perfect example of 'everything old is new again'. Built in the 19th century by British brothers-in-law William Gooderham and James Worts, these 75 buildings on 5.3ha (13 acres) of prime downtown land became the largest distillery in the British Empire. It closed in 1990 and stood deserted until just a few years ago when it reinvented itself as a Victorian-era jewel, filled with chic restaurants, art galleries, studios and theatres, complete with jazz bands, oyster bars and outdoor barbecues.

55 Mill Street. Tel: (416) 203-2121. www.thedistillerydistrict.com

Gardiner Museum of Ceramic Art

Located directly across the street from the ROM, this is the first museum of

Downtown Toronto at dawn

throughout the year – with lessons in sailing during the summer and sessions in ice skating during the winter. The **Queens Quay Terminal**, at the eastern corner of the harbourfront area, is a glittering palace of commercialism. *York Quay Centre, 235 Queens Quay West (at York Quay). Tel: (416) 973-4000. www.harbourfrontcentre.com*

Ontario Place (OP)

This theme park/entertainment centre was created more than 30 years ago as a massive complex of rides, slides, restaurants and concert halls on three man-made islands. OP is known during the day for its Children's Village and water theme park (it is the best babysitter in the city) and at night for the musical concerts at the Molson Amphitheatre and packed cafés, pubs and restaurants. *955 Lake Shore Boulevard West. Tel: (416) 314-9900. www.ontarioplace.com. Open: May–Sept, daily from 10am. Admission charge to park. Children's season pass (charge).*

ceramic art ever to be built in North America. And, like the ROM, it has become so popular that it also underwent an expansion, adding on another 930sq m (10,000sq ft) of exhibition space. The collections are dazzling and delicate, with age-old samples of ceramics from Europe and Asia, and even a large collection of pre-Columbian artefacts. *111 Queens Park (at Bloor Street). Tel: (416) 586-8080. www.gardinermuseum.on.ca. Open: daily 10am–6pm. Admission charge.*

Harbourfront Centre

This 'play-and-parks' stretch along the Toronto waterfront is home to arts and theatre companies, galleries and museums, working artists (you can watch the glassblowers work around their fiery kilns from the safety of an elevated walkway) and working writers – who read from selected works

Royal Ontario Museum (ROM)

The ROM, Toronto's version of the Louvre or the British Museum, has had a multi-million-dollar facelift which has brought it into the 21st century. This museum contains a little bit of everything, including displays on mankind's natural and cultural development, a huge Chinese collection of artefacts, the Indigenous People's collections, as well as dinosaurs and mummies for the kids.

100 Queens Park, at Bloor Street.
Tel: (416) 586-8000.
www.rom.on.ca. Open: daily 10am–9pm.
Admission charge.

St Lawrence Market

On a Saturday, this is one of the most crowded (and fun) buildings you will find in the city; it is packed from very early morning (some experienced shoppers actually get there at 5am when the market opens) to late afternoon. All produce, fruit, meat, seafood – any type of food you want – is guaranteed to be the freshest of the fresh. The little cafés, fast-food stands and cooking wares are in the basement level. Many join the queue and patiently wait to order a breakfast of thick back bacon on a bun plus a coffee, or wait even longer for the unique slow-roasted, specially spiced chicken sandwiches and fries from Churrasco of St Lawrence. You will definitely need to stock up on their addictive creamy Portuguese custard tarts.
92 Front Street East at Jarvis Street.
Tel: (416) 392-7219.

CITY OF NEIGHBOURHOODS

There are more nationalities, cultures, religions and cuisines in Toronto than in any other city around the globe. In fact, the United Nations has officially declared Toronto to be 'the most ethnically diverse city in the world'. The areas are well defined with 'neighbourhood' signs right under the official street name.

The Beach

This neighbourhood consists of a single street chock-a-block with restaurants, bars and pubs, souvenir shops, trendy fashion, leather goods, and anything else that draws a summer crowd to any little beach town, including an area of green parkland and golden sand separated by a 6-km ($3^1/_2$-mile) wooden boardwalk and paved path for bikers or rollerbladers.
The Beach starts at Woodbine Avenue and stretches east several kilometres along Queen Street to the end of the streetcar line.

The popular Beach boardwalk

Toronto

Chinatown

There are five Chinatowns in the Greater Toronto Area but the main one, along Spadina Avenue, is the most popular and accessible. The street is always bustling with colour and movement; stunning silk blouses of red and gold adorn one shop window while its neighbour features Peking duck hanging on a butcher's hook. Countless noodle restaurants sell a huge bowl of aromatic and spicy delights to the hungry crowd (a filling lunch is inexpensive) while the herb shops still sell ancient roots and potions that have kept the Chinese healthy for thousands of years.

The city's main Chinatown starts at Yonge Street and stretches west to Spadina Avenue and then up and down Spadina.

Bustling street in Chinatown

Church & Wellesley (the 'Gay Ghetto')

Right between downtown's Yonge Street and the renovated glory of old Cabbagetown mansions is the very vibrant area know locally as 'the Gay Ghetto'. (And no, this is not a slur. In fact, Toronto is one of the most popular cities in Canada for gay marriages.) This downtown enclave has become the home and meeting place for most of the local and visiting gay and lesbian crowd. Of course, heterosexuals are welcome too; in Toronto no one really cares about your sexual orientation. The bars, cafés and restaurants along Church Street are fun and unpretentious and open to everyone. *The city's self-proclaimed 'Gay Ghetto' starts at Bloor Street and heads straight down Church Street to Queen Street in the south. The corner of Church and Wellesley is the main hub of activity.*

The Danforth (Greektown)

It is easy to believe you are visiting the Plakka in Athens if you sit at an outdoor café along the Danforth, sipping *ouzo*, eating *souvlaki* and hearing nothing but Greek spoken by all those passing by. This is the largest Greek neighbourhood in North America, a true enclave of Greek culture and custom, with authentic cuisine with old-style recipes from Athens and the Aegean. If you really want the inside scoop on the area (where to go, what to see), stop at the Detroit Diner (there is a large Greek population in that US city as well) and speak to 'Mr Chris'.

Toronto's Greektown runs about eight blocks along Danforth Avenue between Broadview and Pape Avenue in the east.

The Entertainment District

The transformation in this downtown area has been astounding – the street has gone from a display of old dingy storefronts and warehouses to a glitzy district of media, theatre, film and sports. The arts attractions include the Royal Alexandria Theatre (a lovingly restored grande theatre from the Victorian age), the new multi-million-dollar 2,200-seat Princess of Wales Theatre and the Roy Thomson Hall, home of the Toronto Symphony Orchestra. The Canadian Opera Company and National Ballet of Canada recently moved to a new venue – the Four Seasons Centre for the Performing Arts – a few blocks north at Queen and University.

Sports fans can take delight in the fact that Toronto is the only North American city to claim four major league sports franchises that play in two downtown stadiums within a few blocks of each other. Hockey's Toronto Maple Leafs and basketball's Toronto Raptors play at the Air Canada Centre (ACC), while baseball's Toronto Blue Jays and football's Toronto Argonauts claim the Rogers Centre (formerly the SkyDome) as their home.

This is an eight-block area that starts at Yonge Street and runs west along

Rogers Centre – home to the Toronto Blue Jays

King Street to Bathurst, then south to Harbourfront.

Leslieville

One of the up-and-coming districts of Toronto is also the home of the city's television and film industry; huge warehouses and sound studios stretch along both Eastern Avenue and the Lakeshore. The main thoroughfare, along Queen Street East, is 'a neighbourhood in transition' – meaning that a new up-market restaurant is located right beside a run-down laundromat. This was always a slightly tired area, stuck between downtown and the trendy Beach, and there has been very little change or renovation in the past 50 years. However, the area's first Starbuck's recently opened at the corner of Logan

Avenue (right next to the hot and spicy offerings from Cajun Corner) which means the neighbourhood has officially been discovered and is now on an upward trajectory.

The area is known for its second-hand furniture stores, the new art galleries, old-style pubs and neighbourhood restaurants.

Leslieville runs along Queen Street East between De Grassi Street and Leslie.

Little Italy

This is one of the most colourful – and often noisiest – neighbourhoods in the city. But it is a good noise – friendly and inviting. Sit at any of the little pavement cafés (Café Diplomatico, or 'The Dip', is the centre of it all) and watch the passing parade along College Street.

The main Italian section stretches along College Street between Bathurst and Shaw.

Little Italy

Queen Street West

Queen of Cool – the street is filled with restaurants, bars, trendy shopping and a plethora of nightclubs that are packed every night of the week. There are dozens of clubs along the parallel streets of Richmond and Adelaide; former warehouses that have undergone multi-million-dollar renovations. Anchoring the area is the **CITY-TV** building (299 Queen Street West) a Mecca for the young and hip, home to Canada's MuchMusic and Bravo speciality television networks.

The trendy nightclub/bar scene of Queen West can be found between University Avenue and Bathurst Street.

TORONTO ENVIRONS
Black Creek Pioneer Village

This village is a perfectly preserved little enclave of the early 19th century, located on the outskirts of the city. The illusion that you have been transported back to the Strong family farm, circa 1816, is challenged only by looking above the treetops at the 20th-century apartment buildings looming overhead. The Village is an authentic re-creation of 30 buildings that were all collected from around the province – complete with blacksmith shop, where the smithy still shoes horses, and the village bakery, which produces hot, homemade breads throughout the day.

1000 Murray Ross Parkway. Tel: (416) 736-1733. www.bcpvinfo@trca.on.ca. Open: Tue–Sun 10am–5pm. Closed: Mon. Admission charge.

McMichael Canadian Art Collection

The world's largest log cabin was built to house the largest collection of paintings from Canada's world-renowned Group of Seven. These seven artists (Tom Thomson, A Y Jackson, Lawren Harris, A J Casson, Franklin Carmichael, F H Varley and Emily Carr) were known for depicting the Canadian landscape from coast to coast in vibrant colours.

Islington Avenue in the town of Kleinberg, about 45 minutes from downtown Toronto. Tel: (905) 893-1121. www.mcmichael.com. Open: daily 10am–4pm. Admission charge.

Paramount Canada's Wonderland

This is the city's major theme park, with rides, slides and dizzying roller-coaster thrills – in fact, the park boasts a total of nine different roller-coaster trips for the addicts of heart-stopping thrills. There are more than 40 theme rides throughout the park, with more being added every season, as well as a 16-ha (40-acre) park called Splashworks just for water activities, including one with an eight-storey drop. There are other, more sedate sections of the park as well, such as the Broadway-type shows for kids at the Paramount Theatre and the Kingswood Concert Theatre in the evening for adult music lovers.

9580 Jane Street (Highway 400 north of Toronto to Rutherford Road). Tel: (905) 832-7000.

Black Creek Pioneer Village

www.canadas-wonderland.com. Open: May–Oct daily 9am–11pm. Admission charge.

Toronto Metro Zoo

This 287-ha (710-acre) zoological park, located on the northeastern fringes of the city, is home to at least 5,000 animals from every corner of the globe. Some 600 species are presented in their perfectly replicated natural habitats, all climate-controlled, and filled with the flora and fauna of Africa, China. Eurasia and the Americas. There are four major pavilions and numerous outdoor ranges throughout the zoo.

Meadowvale Road north of Highway 401 East. Tel: (416) 392-5929. www.torontozoo.com. Open: daily 9am–7pm. Admission charge.

The Toronto film industry

Lights! Camera! Action! There is a lot of cinematic action in this city that has been dubbed 'Hollywood North'. There are actually more feature films, television shows and music videos filmed in Toronto than in any other city in North America.

It is impossible to drive anywhere in the city without seeing dozens of huge production vans parked along the streets with plenty of civilian gawkers trying to get a glimpse of who-knows-what film star.

Statistics released by the city revealed that in 2005 alone there were a total of 1,258 film projects in the Toronto area that generated approximately $900 million dollars in annual revenues. It is estimated that some 25,000 people work in the film industry, making this one of the largest employers in Toronto.

City 'double'

Toronto often replaces and replicates large American cities including New York, Chicago and Boston in films ranging from the Oscar-winning musical *Chicago* and the Depression-era boxing drama *Cinderella Man* to the modern-day drama of *Good Will Hunting*. In addition, the city has also acted as a 'stand-in' for Britain, Israel, Russia and France – the timeless architecture of the city makes this a perfect location for many period pieces, specifically those set in the 1920s and 1930s.

Famous residents

Toronto has a reputation for welcoming well-known actors and allowing them to just hang out – most people simply nod and acknowledge their presence. It is rare to have a fan approach someone for an autograph.

It means that superstar actors including Richard Gere, Catherine Zeta-Jones, Russell Crowe, Renee Zellweger, Matt Damon, Ben Affleck and Robin Williams are happy to make Toronto their home for part of the year and just wander around shopping and dining like regular folk.

Toronto International Film Festival

All of this activity makes Toronto the perfect location to create a legendary film festival. The 'little film festival that could' started 30 years ago when visionaries Bill Marshall and Dusty Cohl started bringing in international films and renting cinemas on their personal credit cards. Today the Toronto International Film Festival

(TIFF) is the largest public film festival in the entire world. For ten days every September, hundreds of thousands of film lovers, movie stars, film executives and international media flock to the more than 350 films and countless parties when the world's film industry comes to Toronto.

There are two gala red-carpet premiers every night as dozens of theatres all over the city screen films every day from 10am to special midnight showings. Many people order the (huge) annual film catalogue in advance and plan annual holidays around their personal film schedules. It is nirvana for film fans and celebrity watchers – especially since various bars receive a special 4am last call during the festival.

You will see every star in town at one time or another at Bistro 990 on Bay Street directly across from the Sutton Place hotel. This is always party central. Many Hollywood types will also stay at the Four Seasons and Park Plaza (in Yorkville) and can usually be found shopping along the trendy and expensive stretch of Bloor Street between Yonge Street and Spadina Avenue. Simply keep your eyes open for Jack Nicholson or Helen Mirren.

Toronto International Film Festival Group. 2 Carlton Street, suite 1600. Tel: (416) 967-7371 or (416) 968-FILM. www.tiffg.ca

The Toronto International Film Festival takes place in Roy Thomson Hall

Walk: The Toronto Islands

The Toronto Islands, a series of little islands connected by bridges and walkways, sit smack dab in the middle of Toronto Harbour. This walk and/or bike ride will take you through parklands, boardwalks, beaches (one is clothing optional), yacht clubs, picnic tables and barbecues, garden restaurants and a community of homes, a mere seven-minute ferry ride from the hustle and bustle of Toronto's urban core. Except for service vehicles, the area is a car-free zone.

Ferry timetable. Tel: (416) 392-8193.

Allow: three hours or all day.

Begin at the Toronto Island Ferry Terminal just behind the Westin Harbour Castle Hotel at the foot of Yonge Street and the Queen's Quay. Take the ferry to Ward's Island.

1 Ward's Island

This eastern island is a small community of 600 residents who live in (mainly) beautiful little cottage-type homes, often reminiscent of a Cape Cod village. The 'locals' are used to visitors and are happy to discuss their island lifestyle with envious day-trippers.
Head south.

2 The Rectory Café

This restaurant (on Ward's Island) is the best spot for food on the Islands. Open year-round, it boasts a beautiful garden setting with a menu featuring goodies such as homemade aubergine sandwiches and freshly grilled lamb burgers. The bulletin board lists all the social/music/arts events happening on the Islands.
Continue along the same road, passing St Andrews Church.

3 Boat and bike rentals

The signs will point the way as you walk west on Ward's Island. Bicycles, tandems, even a four-seater quad for a family, are all available to rent. For those who wish to paddle around the island lagoons and discover all the little curves and coves, yachts and houseboats, you can rent a canoe or a rowing boat.
Walk across the bridge to Centre Island.

4 Centreville

This 8-ha (20-acre) theme park, located on Centre Island, is aimed at families and kids with rides, water slides, an antique car and train rides, and an 18-hole mini-golf course all in the context of an early 20th-century Ontario village. Both a full-day ride pass for those under 1.2m (4ft) tall or a family pass are available.

Return to Ward's Island and turn right on Lakeshore Avenue.

5 Manitou Beach

The main swimming and sunbathing beach is popular and often packed with picnicking families, children from summer-school day camps and teenagers looking to escape the city heat. Protected by a breakwater, this is like paddling in a warm, shallow wading pool.

Continue on Lakeshore Avenue.

6 Hanlon's Point Clothing Optional Beach

The city's only officially sanctioned nude beach, on the western side of the island, is a secluded stretch mainly frequented by the gay set.

Carry on through the park to the ferry terminal near the Ned Hanlan statue. This will take you back to the city.

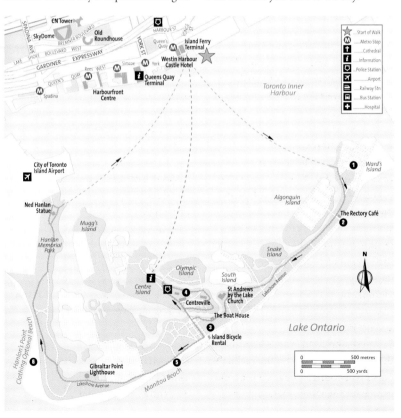

★	....Start of Walk
Ⓜ	.....Metro Stop
✝	....Cathedral
ⓘ	....Information
Ⓞ	...Police Station
✈	....Airport
▤	...Railway Stn
▤	...Bus Station
✚	........Hospital

CN Tower
SkyDome
Old Roundhouse
SPADINA AVE
BREMNER BOULEVARD
LAKE SHORE BOULEVARD WEST
GARDINER EXPRESSWAY
QUEEN'S QUAY
HARBOUR ST
YORK ST
YONGE ST
Queen's Quay
Rees WEST
Simcoe
York
Spadina
Harbourfront Centre
Queens Quay Terminal
Westin Harbour Castle Hotel
Island Ferry Terminal
Toronto Inner Harbour
City of Toronto Island Airport
Ward's Island
Ned Hanlan Statue
Mugg's Island
Algonquin Island
The Rectory Café
Hanlan Memorial Park
Snake Island
Olympic Island
Centre Island
Centreville
South Island
St Andrews by the Lake Church
The Boat House
Island Bicycle Rental
Lakeshore Avenue
Lake Ontario
N
Hanlon's Point Clothing Optional Beach
Gibraltar Point Lighthouse
Lakeshore Avenue
Manitou Beach

0	500 metres
0	500 yards

Niagara Falls and environs

Every year millions of visitors come to Niagara to witness one of the acknowledged natural wonders of the world – the truly awesome sight of a raging river turning into a roaring waterfall.

So powerful is the water rushing over the 49-m (162-ft) drop of the Horseshoe Falls that you will hear the crashing and see the billowing mists long before the Falls come into view. *Niagara Falls Canada Visitor and Convention Bureau. 5433 Victoria Avenue, Niagara Falls. Tel: (800) 563-255 or (905) 356-6061. www.tourismniagara.com/nfcvcb*

Clifton Hill

The City of Niagara Falls seems to have cultivated its own little area of tacky fun along Clifton Hill. The area is only a few blocks away from the American Falls, straight up the hill, and is filled with brightly coloured (or garish, depending on your point of view) attractions such as The Haunted House, The Mystery Maze, the disturbingly lifelike historical and murderous figures at Tussaud's Waxworks, celebrity mannequins in the Movieland Museum of Stars, Ripley's Believe It or Not, Guinness Museum of World Records and

even the House of Frankenstein. *www.cliftonhill.com*

Horseshoe Falls

First of all, try and avoid summer weekends in Niagara: the city is

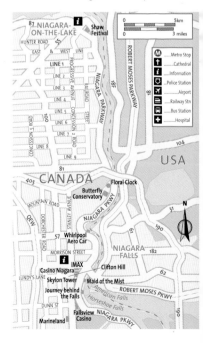

absolutely jammed. Book a visit midweek instead. However, there will always be crowds packed into the viewing area at the Table Rock site, no matter when you visit. The Horseshoe Falls are unique in that you can stand at the very edge of the Falls, just 1m (3ft) away from the thundering water, as it crashes 49m (162ft) straight down into the churning whirlpool at the bottom at the astonishing rate of 152,920cu m (200,000cu ft) of water per second. You may have to squirm through the crowd to get into position by the strong stone-and-iron railing, but it is well worth the hassle. Have your camera ready.

Journey behind the Falls

While at the Table Rock Complex, which includes a second-level restaurant overlooking the Falls (window seats are at a premium), snack bar and souvenir shops on the ground level, join the crowd taking an elevator down 38m (125ft) through solid rock for a walk behind the Falls. Visitors don yellow rain slickers for a misty stroll through the tunnel that leads to several outlooks directly behind the torrent of cascading waters. There is also an outdoor observation deck at the side where you can watch the thundering waters literally smash into the gorge.

Niagara Falls and environs

Niagara Falls in winter

You have to know you are going to get wet in Niagara.
Table Rock. Tel: (905) 354-1551. www.niagaraparks.com. Open: daily 9am–6pm. Admission charge.

Maid of the Mist

This is a must for any visitor to Niagara (there will be a queue, but it is worth the wait for this once-in-a-lifetime thrill ride). If the sight of this little boat being bounced around hasn't made you too anxious, your next stop will be to queue for tickets just opposite the American Falls. Unfortunately, you cannot book in advance, so prepare for a lengthy line-up. (Note: the crowds are much smaller in the morning – first cruise leaves at 9.45am.)

The little ship chugs past the American Falls and Cave of the Winds before it charges straight into the massive semicircle of water.
5920 River Road. Tel: (905) 358-5781. www.maidofthemist.com. Open: daily May–Oct 9am–7pm. Admission charge.

Marineland

This is one of the city's most popular attractions. The marine show features killer whales, sea lions and leaping dolphins, plus there's a wilderness zoo with elk, buffaloes and bears. Of course, as the name implies, there are also plenty of wet and wild water rides for the kids, as well as restaurants, picnic areas and a nearby campsite. Many families come to Niagara for the day and never do get to see those famous Falls.

8375 Stanley Avenue, Niagara Falls. Tel: (905) 356-8250. www.marinelandcanada.com. Open: daily May–Oct 9am–7pm. Numerous tickets and passes available.

Niagara Park Butterfly Conservatory

This is located about 8km (5 miles) from the Falls itself along the Niagara Parkway and just south of the Floral Clock (a massive clock made of plants and flowers right beside the parkway). This colourful conservatory dazzles the guest with thousands of live exotic butterflies from around the globe. It is an absolute riot of rainbow colours in a lush, climate-controlled, 1,023sq m (11,000sq ft) tropical environment.
Niagara Parkway. Tel: (905) 356-8119. www.niagaraparks.com. Open: daily 9am–7pm. Admission charge.

Niagara casinos

Since the first casino appeared in Niagara a few years ago, the city has discovered another type of tourist – single-minded individuals, millions of them, who head directly for a gambling emporium and miss the Falls entirely. For this group, the casinos are the only places in town.
Casino Niagara. 5705 Falls Avenue. Tel: 888-WINFALL or (905) 946-3255. www.casinoniagara.com
The Fallsview Casino. 6380 Fallsview Blvd. Tel: 888-FALLSVUE. www.fallsviewcasinoresort.com

Niagara Falls Imax Theatre and Daredevil Adventure

This showcases the largest collection of barrels and homemade contraptions used by daredevils who have challenged the Falls. Some survived; some didn't. Those who want the free-floating experience of tipping over the edge, without getting wet, can watch a video filmed through the window of a barrel. *6170 Buchanan Avenue. Tel: (905) 374-4629. www.nfimax@niagara.com. Open: daily 10am–8pm. Admission charge.*

Skylon Tower

The best overview (unless you book a helicopter ride) for photographing the Falls is from the Skylon Tower; the little 'yellow bug' exterior elevators will zoom you up some 236m (775ft) to the indoor/outdoor Observation Deck. This will give you another spectacular perspective of one of the world's greatest wonders.
5200 Robinson Street. Tel (800) 814-9577. www.skylon.com. Open: daily 8am–midnight. Admission charge.

Whirlpool Aero Car

This aerial ride, just a little downstream from the Falls, will allow you to swing into space in an open-air gondola overlooking the raging turbulence of the whirlpool far below. You won't require your passports because the car runs between two Canadian points only, not across the gorge to the USA. The aero car is only operational in the summer months, and even then it depends on
Continued on p46.

Niagara Falls and environs

The perfectly preserved Apothecary Museum in Niagara

Ontario wineries and vineyards

Ontario's Golden Horseshoe, the agricultural arc extending from Toronto to Niagara, has always been known for its farmlands and fruit orchards – this region promotes its world-famous cucumbers, pumpkins, apples, peaches, strawberries and, fortunately, grapes.

And though the country has a hard-won reputation as a nation of hockey-watching beer drinkers, over the past few decades Ontarians have discovered that they like their grapes in liquid form, preferably with a five-star meal.

Fortunately, the warming influence of Lake Ontario – combined with the protective ridge of the looming Niagara Escarpment – mirrors a climate similar to other wine-producing areas of the world, such as Burgundy, the Loire Valley and New Zealand.

As a result, dozens of wineries have sprung up in the past 25 years to create a world-renowned industry with wines that have won prizes of gold, silver and bronze on the international Olympic stage of Wine Production. Of particular note are the Ontario Icewines, a speciality created from the frosty weather of the late autumn harvest.

The vineyards can be seen along Queen Elizabeth Way (QEW) Niagara highway as you pass by the numerous fruit stands outside the towns of

Niagara-on-the-Lake's Pillitteri Estates Winery

Grimsby, Beamsville, Jordan and the appropriately named Vineland Station.

Ontario has been producing wine for some 200 years, but it had the reputation of being inexpensive 'plonk' for the masses. This was partially due to the fact that the few wineries were hampered by government regulations forcing them to use the very harsh and acidic indigenous Lambrusca grape. These laws changed in the late 1970s and independent winegrowers were allowed to use classic varietal grapes. These experimental blends added various new tastes and textures to the mix. For those unfamiliar with Ontario wines, always look for the Vintners Quality Alliance (VQA) label.

The major wine/vineyard event of the year is the celebration of the autumn harvest during the annual **Niagara Grape & Wine Festival** (Tel: (905) 688-0212. www.niagaraicewinefestival.com). This late September/early October grapefest (the dates change slightly every year) features more than 100 events including tours and tastings, concerts and seminars, cuisine and, well, more tastings.

Wine Council of Ontario. 11 Hanover Drive, St Catharines. www.wineroute.com

Most of the wineries promote their product with tours and wine tastings from May to October. Check in

The Henry of Pelham Estate Winery

advance for a specific winery you may wish to visit, but the following have regular tours and impressive wines.

The Cave Spring Cellars 3836 Main Street, Jordan. Tel: (905) 562-3581. www.cavespringcellars.com

Château des Charmes Wines 1025 York Road, Niagara-on-the-Lake. Tel: (905) 262-4219.

The Henry of Pelham Family Estate Winery 1469 Pelham Road, St. Catharines. Tel: (905) 684-8423. www.henryofpelham.com

Inniskillin Wines Niagara Parkway, just outside Niagara-on-the-Lake. Tel: (905) 468-3554. www.inniskillin.com

Jackson-Triggs Niagara Estate 2145 RR 55, Niagara-on-the-Lake. Tel: (905) 468-4637.

Reif Estate Winery 15608 Niagara Parkway, Niagara-on-the-Lake. Tel: (905) 468-7738.

weather and wind conditions. But if you get there on a sunny, windless day, this is an awesome sight.

Tel: (877) 642-7275. www.niagaraparks. com. Open: daily Mar–Nov 9am–7pm. Admission charge.

NIAGARA-ON-THE-LAKE (NOTL)

In 1792, NOTL became the first capital of Upper Canada, later the Province of Ontario, and was a major site in the occasional skirmish against the American forces just across the river. Today this beautifully quaint village is the site of a daily invasion of tourists, busloads of them, who stroll the perfectly preserved 18th-century-style shops and boutiques, stocking up on homemade jams and jellies, extra-rich ice cream, Irish linens and Scottish tweeds, photographing the towering town clock in the middle of Main Street and filling the restaurants and pubs before taking in an afternoon matinee at the Shaw Festival. Council bylaws ensure that any building or store on the main street must conform to the 18th-century style of the village.

Niagara-on-the-Lake Chamber of Commerce/VC. 153 King Street. Tel: (905) 468-1950. www.niagaraonthelake.com

Niagara Apothecary Museum

This little corner 'drug store' museum, perfectly preserved from 1866, sits on the corner right next to the town clock in the middle of the square. The

Casino Niagara is a popular destination

Ontario College of Pharmacists owns and operates this shop and has preserved the feel of an old-time apothecary, complete with a glass jar filled with liquorice for the kids. Note the rare collection of apothecary glass and original walnut counters.

Niagara Apothecary Museum. 5 Queen Street. Tel: (905) 468-3845. Open: daily 10am–5pm.

SHAW FESTIVAL THEATRE

No visit to the Niagara area is complete without experiencing a play or musical at the Shaw. This theatre not only single-handedly revived the world's interest in the Irish playwright – and uncovered other theatrical gems that had been sitting dormant for many years – but also turned the town of Niagara-on-the-Lake into one of the most popular tourist destinations in the province. The theatre's original mandate, to present plays by George Bernard Shaw 'and his contemporaries', was revised a few years ago to include plays and musicals written during the playwright's lifetime. This expanded the company's creative energies to include such varied fare as Cole Porter's *High Society* and Stephen Sondheim's *Gypsy* in repertoire with Shaw's *Major Barbara* and *Pygmalion*.

The Shaw provides an intimate atmosphere for the theatre-lover; the main Festival Theatre has only 856 seats, the Court House stage 327, and the lovely little Royal George, a former movie house, has 328. This has become one of the most respected theatres in the English-speaking world, and actors vie for the opportunity to become part of the permanent company.

An example of what artistic director Jackie Maxwell might offer in one ambitious and diverse season includes productions of Shaw's *Saint Joan* and *The Philanderer*, the Jerry Herman musical *Mack and Mabel*, Brian Friel's *A Month in the Country*, George Feydeau's French farce *Hotel Peccadillo* (*L'hôtel du libre échange*) and the Tennessee Williams drama *Summer and Smoke*.

The Shaw Festival. 10 Queen's Parade. Tel: (800) 657-1106 or (905) 468-2153. www.shawfest.com

Greaves Jams & Marmalades

This little shop sells some of the most delicious jams and jellies you will ever taste; orange, peach, apple, blueberry and, of course, grape, all natural ingredients from the orchards of the Niagara farmers.

55 Queen Street. Tel: (905) 468-7831. www.greavesjams.com. Open: daily 10am–5pm.

Niagara Parkway

The 25-km (15-mile) winding parkway between the Falls and Niagara-on-the-Lake is one of the most beautiful and scenic drives in the province – the entire area is protected greenbelt under the Niagara Parks Commission. This is a leisurely drive past trees and vineyards, golf courses and 18th-century farmhouses, apple orchards and fruit stands along the highway. On the opposite side are plenty of picnic areas and rest stops where you can relax and look over the gorge into the Niagara River, and wave to those across the river in New York State. The best time for a drive along the Parkway is during autumn, when the leaves turn red and gold.

Niagara Parks Commission. Tel: (905) 356-2241. www.niagaraparks.com

Stratford and environs

This quiet little bucolic farming community in Ontario's Perth County changed forever in 1959 when local dreamer Tom Patterson presented the town with an audacious suggestion – since the town was called Stratford perhaps the local council could create a Shakespearean Festival like its namesake in England. Since then, the town has developed into a tourist haven like few others in the province.

It still has a rural setting, but now the town is filled with trendy shops and chic boutiques, fine dining, up-market accommodation, fancy B&Bs, art galleries and mini-nightclubs – all centred around one man's flight of fancy that transformed a sleepy rural community into one of the major destinations for theatre-lovers.

City of Stratford. Box 818, Stratford. Tel: (800) 561-SWAN or (519) 271-5140. www.city.stratford.on.ca

Art in the Park

This outdoor exhibition is definitely a 'weather permitting' activity. From early June to the end of September, local artists and artisans gather to

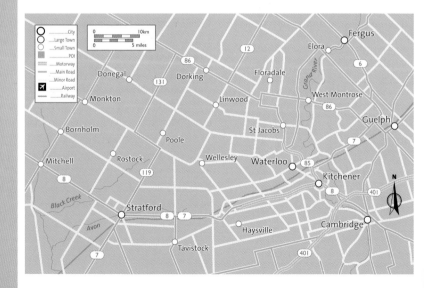

display (and hopefully sell) their paintings and pottery, crafts of leatherwork and glass, jewellery and sculptures, along the banks of the Avon River. The artists from Perth County have gained a reputation over the years for their creativity.
Lakeside Drive and Front Street. Tel: (519) 272-0429. www.artintheparkstratford.com

Avon River

Many people visit Stratford just to picnic along the banks of the Avon River. This is a restful and romantic setting; green parkland and trees, flocks of swans gliding through the waters, and dewy-eyed couples sharing a picnic basket sprawled on a blanket near the banks of the river. You can bring your own basket of goodies or order a 'take-out picnic' from one of the many restaurants in the area. You'll also find many actors in the park, taking a break from rehearsals.

Gallery Stratford

This beautiful little art gallery, with its changing displays of contemporary and traditional art, is located just down the hill and across the park from the main Festival Theatre. There is a permanent section featuring local artists, and a range of work from the pastoral to avant-garde. Revolving exhibitions often display the colourful costume sketches for the creations produced in the seamstress workshop of the Festival.

54 Romeo Street. Tel: (519) 271-5271. www.gallerystratford.com. Open: Tue–Sun 10am–5pm. Closed: Mon. Free admission.

Stratford Strolls

The city offers free guided theme tours during the summer, for example the Historic Tour, Shakespearean Gardens Tour and Art Tour. The times and dates change every year, so check with Tourism Stratford. The city also offers a free 'self-guide' stroll, featuring the main architectural and historic sites such as the 1853 Perth County Courthouse (Queen Anne Revival style), the neoclassical Albion Hotel, built in 1855, and the Gothic Revival 1913 Know Presbyterian Church.
Tourism Stratford Information. York Street, Box 818. Tel: (519) 271-5140. www.city.stratford.on.ca

STRATFORD ENVIRONS
Kitchener-Waterloo/Oktoberfest

The city of Kitchener-Waterloo is known primarily for its annual Oktoberfest celebrations – reportedly the largest outside of Munich. This farming area was settled by 19th-century German immigrants, and although the settlement was initially called Berlin, the people diplomatically voted to change the name to Kitchener at the start of the First World War. Waterloo was a neighbouring farm community and the two just grew into each other.

During the ten-day Oktoberfest of all things German, every social club, beer hall, pub and restaurant – as well as numerous beer tents that sprout up all over town – pay annual homage to the successful autumn crops with a liquid celebration of malt, barley, hops and wheat. This is the town for you if you like heavy, hearty old-style German cooking – you can depend on any restaurant with its name ending in 'haus'. *Kitchener-Waterloo Visitor and Convention Bureau. 2848 King Street East, Kitchener. Tel: (800) 265-6959 or (519) 748-0800. www.kw-visitor.on.ca Oktoberfest. 17 Benton Street. Tel: (519) 576-4267 or (888) 294 HANS (4267). www.oktoberfest.ca*

Waterloo-St Jacobs Railway

This old 1950s streamliner tourist train runs four times daily between St Jacobs and the City of Waterloo. It takes passengers from the heart of a modern 21st-century city through the countryside into the rural past of a 19th-century farming community. *Waterloo Square, Waterloo. Tel: (519) 746-1950. Call for schedules (May–Oct).*

Elora Mill

St Jacobs

This little Mennonite community, where the basic mode of travel is horse-and-buggy, is situated right in the middle of fertile Ontario farmland. The residents are proud of its 'old ways', namely the strong German Mennonite background they brought to Canada and have maintained in spite of all the years of technology; many still forgo electricity in their homes. (Their one concession to modern ways is a very visual 'day-glo' triangle traffic warning sign that they have fixed to the rear of their buggies.) Oh, and you must give 'right-of-way' to the horses, so just park your car as soon as possible.

The community produces some of the finest handcrafted blankets, coats and shirts in the world – items that may all be purchased in the shops and craft studios within the town. The restaurants serve some truly excellent Mennonite-style home-cooked meals ('Food that really schmeks'), and you will find little hotels (Benjamins) and palatial B&Bs (Jacobstettel).

The St Jacobs Farmers' Market/Flea Market/Outlet Mall

This is one of the most truly authentic farmers' country markets you will ever experience. There are hundreds of vendors, indoors and out, with crammed stalls of vegetables and fruit, quality meats and farm-made cheese, as well as delicious pies and cakes baked with old-world Mennonite secret ingredients. Adjoining the market, shoppers have their choice of discovering 'pre-loved' treasures in the massive flea market or the trendy new boutiques of the St Jacobs Outlet Mall. *Farmers' Market. 878 Weber Street North. Tel: (519) 747-1830. Open: year-round Tue and Sun 8am–3pm (June–Sept daily from 8am). St Jacobs Outlet Mall. 25 Benjamin Road East. Tel: (519) 888-0138. www.stjacobs.com. Open: daily 9am–8pm.*

The Mennonite Story

Conveniently located right in the centre of this little town, making it impossible to miss, is the Meeting Place that tells the story and history of the Old Order of Mennonites in Ontario through old illustrations, photographs, literature and a multimedia production.
St Jacobs Visitors Centre. 1408 King Street West. Tel: (519) 664-3518. www.stjacobs.com. Open: June–Sept 10am–5pm. Admission charge.

Maple Syrup Museum of Ontario

This museum shows the history and production of maple syrup. Those with a sweet tooth will want to visit the Farm Pantry down the street for syrup, candies and fudges.
Country Mill Store. Corner of Front and King streets. Tel: (519) 664-1232. Open: daily 10am–5pm. Free admission.

Elora

This quiet, quaint former mill town on the Elora Gorge has reinvented itself as a small arts-and-crafts community. The 19th-century stone mansions have been renovated to retain the exterior flavour of a bygone era, with modern amenities inside. The little shops bordering the river sell everything from antique furniture and hand-dipped wax candles to homemade sweaters and chic cappuccinos.

The main building is the original 1859 gristmill (**Elora Mill Country Inn**), which is one of the best places in the province for a romantic getaway.

The best time to visit is during the **Elora Music Festival** in July when the community produces a festival of choral arts and classical music using natural venues. For instance, when was the last time you saw singers on a raft in the middle of a gorge? The audience sits around the top of the cliffs, on pillows and blankets, as the natural acoustics of the rock quarry fill the night skies with celestial song.
Tourist Office. 5 Mill Street East. Tel: (519) 846-9841. www.elora.info

Mennonites selling corn in St Jacobs

Stratford Festival

The Stratford Festival is one of the great theatrical success stories of the 20th century. It started under a large canvas tent in a grassy field and turned into the largest classical repertory theatre in North America. Local boy Tom Patterson convinced Sir Michael Langham to become the first artistic director and, oh yes, perhaps he could interest a few of his friends from England to join this great adventure. Join they did, and in 1953 Langham directed *Richard III* with Sir Alec Guiness and Irene Worth on a wooden stage under a hot, humid canvas tent. The Festival has dramatically thrived and expanded over the years, now presenting plays and musicals in four major venues –

the main 1,826-seat world-famous proscenium-arch stage of the Festival Theatre (which replaced the original tent), the downtown Avon Theatre (1,091 seats), the Tom Patterson Theatre (481 seats), and the new Studio Theatre (260 seats) for more experimental projects and original Canadian drama.

The clarion call of trumpets, seemingly mimicking the swans in the Avon River at the bottom of the grassy slopes, summons the audience for every theatrical presentation at the Festival Theatre – just as they did in Shakespeare's day.

Here's a taste of some of the productions – they might include Shakespeare's *King Lear*, *The Merchant of Venice* and *A Comedy of Errors*, Rodgers and Hammerstein's musical *Oklahoma*, the Gershwins' *My One and Only*, Oscar Wilde's *An Ideal Husband* and Edward Albee's *A Delicate Balance*.

A weekend of world-class drama, comedy and music in this lovely little rural Ontario town is the highlight of the summer

The Avon Theatre in Stratford

robe as Lear, Sir Laurence Olivier's sword in *Julius Caesar* and even Christopher Plummer's 1920s double-breasted suit as Barrymore (a performance that earned him a Tony Award the following year on Broadway). Many of these costumes are rented out to other theatre and film productions as well – so don't be surprised if you've seen a costume in a period costume film. Unlike some places, you are allowed to take photos.

Festival Theatre backstage tour

Theatre-lovers will love this backstage tour of one of the world's greatest stages. The one-hour tour takes the visitor behind the scenes to witness how the props, wigs and costumes are made by a team of designers and wizards of the sewing machine. This is a fascinating insiders' look at how the onstage magic is created.

Stratford's Festival Theatre

season for many theatre-lovers who book their accommodation a year in advance. Note though the theatres are closed on Mondays.

Costume warehouse tour

This massive warehouse holds some 50,000 costumes and stage props, stored in multi-levelled tiers, which highlight the 54-year history of Stratford through clothing design and stagecraft magic. The grand gowns of the Elizabethan age and armour of Rome can be seen in this tour through the theatre's new state-of-the-art facility; the gown Zoe Caldwell wore as Cleopatra, William Hutt's

Meet the Festival

Throughout the summer months (Wednesdays and Fridays) visitors have the opportunity to meet the acting company and theatre staff for informal discussions in both the Tom Patterson and Studio theatres. There is no admission fee, but you must check with the box office to reserve your seat.
Tel: (800) 567-1600 or (519) 271-4040. www.stratfordfestival.ca

Cottage Country

The vast, sprawling and beautiful wilderness north of Toronto is known simply as 'Cottage Country' – the combined holiday area of three tourist regions: Georgian Bay, The Muskokas and Haliburton. You know you are in Cottage Country when you see signposts with names such as Honey Harbour, Big Chute, Bala, Windemere and Rosseau. The four-season playground area stretches from Barrie in the south to Algonquin Park in the north. This is a rural idyll of little villages, lakeside resorts, sailing boats and waterskiing, waterfront mansions and trailer parks, as well as some of the finest resorts and country inns anywhere in the world.

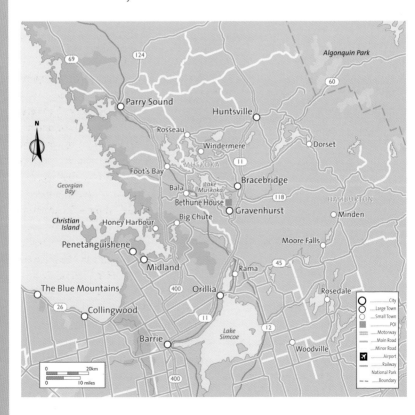

Cottage Country is also a winter wonderland of ski resorts, snowmobiling, dog sledding and just curling up beside the fireplace of your hillside chalet with a hot toddy. Warning: from the 24 May holiday weekend to September's Labour Day, there is a mass exodus northbound from Toronto every Friday afternoon. *Resorts Ontario, PO Box 2148. Orillia. Tel: (800) 363-7227. www.resorts-ontario.com.*
Muskoka. Tel. (800) 267-9700. www.discovermuskoka.ca

Orillia
Weber's

For many, the first sign of summer is the requisite stop at Weber's, a hamburger/hotdog/fries stand along Highway 11 just north of Orillia. Actually 'stand' isn't quite the right word, since this little burger place is made up of railway carriages. Weber's became so popular that 25 years ago the owners built a bridge (from the CN Tower in Toronto) across the highway and developed a 0.4-ha (1-acre) parking lot for the southbound traffic. *Weber's. Highway 11, north of Orillia. Tel: (705) 325-3696. www.webersrestaurants.com*

Collingwood and environs
Blue Mountain Ski Resort

With 34 trails winding down from the top of the Niagara Escarpment range, Blue Mountain is the premier ski resort in the province. During the winter

Blue Mountain

season, the resort is open seven days (and nights) a week, and 21 trails open for night skiing until 10pm. Blue Mountain has designed slopes for every level of skier, from the gentle beginner slopes ('bunny hills') to the thrills of the double black diamond runs.

Blue Mountain also has the largest ski school in the province, both for novices and those who need a 'tune-up' at the start of each season. Don't have your own equipment? The resort has a vast array of skis, poles and boots. Need a new fancy ski outfit? Look no further than their ski boutique.

The view from the top of the escarpment overlooks the magnificent sweep of Georgian Bay – but you can also see it in summer. Blue Mountain is a four-season resort with full accommodation ranging from rented

hillside chalets to full-amenities motel rooms.
RR 3 Collingwood. Tel: (705) 445-0231.
www.bluemountain.ca

Midland
Sainte-Marie-among-the-Hurons

This historic Canadian site, along with the Martyr's Shrine, marks the original establishment of a settlement built by Jesuit missionaries in the 17th century. The native Huron tribe readily accepted their new neighbours – in fact many of the Indians converted to Christianity. This was the site of the first church, hospital, blacksmith shop and farm in the province. These days the many costumed guides in this historical community will take a break from their daily chores in the blacksmith shop or barnyard to answer questions about their little community.

The Martyr's Shrine, just across the road, is a church dedicated to eight Catholic missionaries who were massacred some 350 years ago by a different native tribe who feared the invaders to their land.
Highway 12, east of Midland.
Tel: (705) 526-7838.
Martyr's Shrine. Tel: (705) 526-3788.
www.jesuits.ca/martyrs-shrine-midland
Midland/Penetanguishene. Chamber of Commerce, 2 Main Street, Penetanguishene, Ontario L9M 1T1.
Tel: (705) 549-2232 or (800) 263-7745.
www.georgianbaytourism.com

Wye Marsh Wildlife Centre

Naturalists will need most of the day to

The Martyr's Shrine in Midland

explore the 60-ha (150-acre) protected parklands of this wildlife centre. There are 8km (5 miles) of hiking trails for closer observations of flora and fauna. Don't miss the wobbly stroll along the floating boardwalk through the marshlands.
Across from the Martyr's Shrine.
Tel: (705) 526-7809.
www.wyemarsh.com

Penetanguishene
Discovery Harbour

Just a few miles away in Penetanguishene, take some time to wander along the waterside boardwalks of this re-created 19th-century British naval base. These historic properties are also the site of the replicas of the HMS *Tecumseth* and HMS *Bee*, both of which sail on selected days, and the King's Wharf Theatre offers year-round live entertainment. This is also a good spot to stop for lunch or a snack at one of the dockside pubs.

93 Jury Drive. Tel: (705) 549-8064. www.discoveryharbour.on.ca

Penetanguishene 30,000 Island Cruise

This operates from early May until Canadian Thanksgiving (second Monday in October). You can board the MS *Georgian Queen* right at the dock in the town and cruise through the lush, scenic 30,000 islands for an hour or all day, depending on the schedules. There are also special cruises with music and entertainment, although, for most people, the lush island scenery alone is well worth the price of admission.

Main Street. Tel: (800) 363-7447 or (705) 549-7795). www.georgianbaycruises.com

Gravenhurst

Bethune Memorial House National Historic Site

This restored 1890s home, now a National Historic Site, marks the birthplace of Dr Norman Bethune, who is known in the medical community for his innovative techniques and inventions of surgical instruments – notably the mobile blood transfusion service that he developed on the battlefields during the Spanish Civil War. Bethune became a hero to the Chinese people when he devoted his services to saving their wounded soldiers. He is buried in China and his revered status in that country has helped shaped Canada's reputation as a humanitarian nation.

235 John Street, Gravenhurst, off Highway 169. Tel: (705) 687-4261. www.pc.gc.ca/bethune

Gravenhurst Opera House

This is an amazing structure in the middle of small-town Ontario: an opera house that has been fully restored to its 1901 architectural elegance. The heritage building, a landmark in the province, is known for its perfect acoustics and old-world grandeur. The Opera House hosts musical productions, touring shows and local theatre groups.

295 Muskoka Road S, Gravenhurst. Tel: (705) 687-5550. www.gravenhurst.ca

Muskoka Steamships

This is probably the most popular tourist attraction in Cottage Country – cruising through the Muskoka lakes on board an old-time 19th-century steamship. There are now three ships that sail between 1 June and mid-October: the *Wanda II*, the newly constructed *Wenonah II* and the original 1887 fully restored RMS *Segwun* – the oldest operating coal-fired steamship in North America. There are a number of cruises available to the public – lasting between one and eight hours – it's best to book early for the ever-popular Dinner and Twilight cruises.

Muskoka Wharf, Gravenhurst. Tel: (705) 687-6667. www.muskokasteamships.com

Muskoka Wharf

This recent $170-million addition to the Gravenhurst harbour is a heritage-based attraction that provides a showcase for the history as well as the future development of the Muskoka area. This 36-ha (89-acre) theme park boasts a new baseball diamond, basketball court, outdoor skating rink, yacht basin, luxury hotel, condo developments, restaurants and bars, shops and galleries.

Gravenhurst. Tel: (705) 687-2240.
www.muskokawharf.ca

Muskoka Wildlife Centre

Bears, cougars, even wolverines – you can expect to see all these animals, and more, while walking along the hiking trails of this interactive wildlife centre. There are 40ha (100 acres) of rustic Muskoka landscape (especially beautiful with the changing leaves of the autumn season) here. The guides offer special activities where the guest can 'howl with the wolves' during an evening stroll in the bush. The animals, by the way, are kept securely behind the Plexiglas panels.

Severn Bridge, Gravenhurst.
Tel: (705) 689-0222.
www.muskokawildlifecentre.com

The Town of Rama
Casino Rama

This was Ontario's first casino and the only First Nations commercial casino in the province. The casino is open 24 hours a day, seven days a week – in other words, you can lose your money any time of day or night. There are more than 2,100 ringing slot machines, 120 gaming tables, 7 restaurants and a Las Vegas-style 5,000-seat theatre featuring some of the top musical acts in today's world of entertainment. Dozens of bus tours depart daily from the Greyhound Bus Terminal in Toronto, but you can also stay at the Casino's 300-room, all-suite hotel.

Tel: (705) 329-3325.
www.casinorama.com

Algonquin Provincial Park

This is the big one for lovers of nature. Located on the southern edge of the Canadian Shield, Algonquin encompasses more than 7,725sq km

The hotel lobby at Casino Rama

(3,000sq miles) of wilderness, lakes, rivers, cliffs and beaches. This is a paradise for campers and canoeists; the perfect escape for city dwellers who need to occasionally de-stress from the urban angst.

The park, located about 275km (175 miles) north of Toronto, lists eight official campsites with a total of 1,248 serviced pitches. However, those paddling through the wilderness lakes can simply pitch their tent along countless kilometres of shoreline. There are unlimited canoe routes through the park and many people spend their entire summer vacation 'roughing it in the bush'.

But always remember, you are in the middle of nowhere and various bears and wolves have first claim on the land.

Lake Muskoka in Gravenhurst

Wilderness campers, please note: check in with the park ranger before you start your excursions in the bush. And make sure you notify them of your departure.

About one million people a year visit Algonquin, and most of those stick to the main Highway 60 – from the west gate at Oxtongue Lake to the Town of Whitney in the east – and simply enjoy the campsites, beaches, picnic areas and interpretive hiking trails along the main highway. There is also the opportunity to explore the Algonquin Interpretive Centre, Logging Museum and wildlife exhibitions in the Algonquin Museum, which are all on this road.

For those who don't relish the thought of pitching a tent – or possibly sharing their morning coffee with an ambling bear – but still want the Algonquin experience, reserve a cabin at Arowhon Pines, a resort lodge (with all the amenities) right in the park on Little Joe Lake. The huge cabins all have cathedral-type ceilings and living-room fireplaces. This is the perfect picture-postcard scenic lakeshore setting.

A visit to the park can be made any time of year (some people do enjoy winter camping!), but the colours in late September are truly spectacular as the maple trees turn brilliant shades of red, gold and yellow.

Whitney, Ontario. Tel: (705) 633-5572.
www.ontarioparks.com or
www.algonquinpark.on.ca

Ontario's South Coast

Since the official 'Cottage Country' in the Muskokas has become so crowded, people have slowly been discovering the more rustic joys of southwestern Ontario. This is a relaxed, uncrowded region of small towns, rich farmlands, resort villages and countless miles of sandy shoreline. The infrastructures of the better-known destinations are starting to fray at the edges with too many cottages and resorts, so visitors can expect Ontario's South Coast to become the province's future summer destination hot spot.

If you want to undertake a long drive through the region, begin at Point Pelee in the south and wind your way east along the coastal roads of the Lake Erie shoreline to Niagara Falls (allow three days for this).
South Coast Tourism Inc. Tel: (800) 699-9038 or (519) 426-1695.
www.ontariosouthcoast.com

Point Pelee
This little island and bird sanctuary is actually the southernmost tip of Canada, yet, surprisingly, Pelee Island shares the same latitude as Northern California. Much of the tiny island (20sq km/8sq miles) is protected parkland and a world-recognised bird sanctuary.

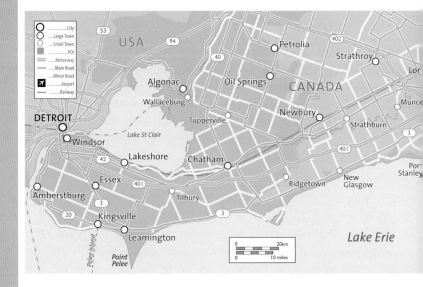

Bird-watchers delight in walking along the wooden walkways deep in the marshland, looking for rare species found only here, such as the Virginia warbler, sage thrasher and even the swallow-tailed kite. This area is a microcosm of mild weather in a cold climate, featuring a flora of Carolina forest and savannah grasslands otherwise unknown in this part of the world. In fact, there are more than 700 species of flowering and non-flowering plant life scattered over the island.

The majority of bird-watchers descend on the island during the annual autumn and spring migration periods. And, for an extra treat, countless thousands of monarch butterflies turn the treetops orange during their October migration to central Mexico.

However, Pelee Island is not just birds and trees. Pelee Island Winery started producing some top Ontario wines (the little winery has the most VQA label wines in the province) in 1979 at their vineyards in Kingsville on the mainland. However, their Wine Pavilion is located on the island and features wine tasting, barbecue lunches and tours around the island.

Boaters can sail to one of Pelee's marinas under their own steam, of course, but most take the daily ferry service from Kingsville or Leamington (Ontario), or Sandusky, Ohio, USA. These 400-passenger, 40-vehicle ferries leave at regularly scheduled times every day (usually 9am from Kingsville to the Island): check for changing times at different periods of the year.

Pelee Island Tourism. 1045 West Shore Road, Pelee Island. Tel (519) 724-2931. www.peleetownship@bellnet.ca

Ontario's South Coast

Pelee Island Winery. Kingsville.
Tel: (519) 733-6551.
www.peleeisland.com
Pelee Island Transportation. Kingsville.
Tel: (519) 724-2115.
www.ontarioferries.com

Point Pelee

Port Stanley

This is a friendly town on the beach, complete with 140-seat summer theatre, restaurants of fine dining and fast food, cosy little B&Bs and cottages to rent, golf courses, tennis courts and a sheltered picturesque marina operated by Transport Canada, a favourite of boaters from both sides of the border. Port Stanley – or simply 'Port' if you want to fit in with the locals – has always been a preferred weekend getaway for resident Ontarians – especially from the nearby (and inland) City of London – but still remains a secret from most of the province. Too bad, because this little lakeside village (formerly called Kettle Creek) is a relaxed getaway from the bustle of big-city living – almost a time warp to a slower-paced way of life. And to emphasise the point, visitors can take a scenic 11-km (7-mile) ride through Elgin County on a 1940s diesel locomotive, courtesy of the Port Stanley Terminal Rail.
Tourist Office. Tel: (519) 631-8188.
www.port-stanley.com

Long Point

This 'town' is basically a 40-km (25-mile) sliver of sand that juts out into Lake Erie and is literally filled with row upon row of cottages along its white sands. A number of people do live here year-round, but this is really a summer spot especially since there are no amenities except a few restaurants and one or two general stores. The closest little town to stock up on supplies is

Port Rowan, a couple of kilometres east along the lakeshore road.

This is a terrific beach resort for families and is always filled with campers in the sandy miles of **Long Point Provincial Park**.

There is no hotel in Long Point but there are plenty of cottages to rent during the season. It is a great place for exercise because once you get off the parallel roads (each one-way only) you will be slogging through sand. Most people on the bay side of this sandy point own boats, and all the marinas are filled for the season.

You cannot drive (the road ends at the provincial park) to the lonely lighthouse at the end of Long Point, or even hike there. This is a protected World Biosphere Reserve and only registered park rangers – and the lighthouse keeper, of course – can get to the tip. The only way to get to the actual point of Long Point is to rent a boat, but even then you are not permitted to step ashore.

Port Rowan-Long Point Chamber of Commerce. Port Rowan. Tel: (519) 586-2201. www.portrowan-longpoint.org

Backus Heritage Conservation Area (NHS)

This old mill, built in 1798, is one of the oldest examples of rural farm life in the province. The Backhouse Mill has been authentically restored and renovated – providing the public with a look at flour production in the 18th century. There is also a re-created Heritage Village on site

– with the actual 1866 Cherry Valley schoolhouse, Backus Family homestead, and museum filled with the history of Norfolk County. Many weddings take place in this romantic pastoral setting (ask to visit the Trista and Simon wedding verandah), with bridal parties gathered around the mill and nearby stream. The historic site is part of the Long Point Region Conservation Authority.

RR 1 Port Rowan. Tel: (519) 586-2201. www.lprca.on.ca/backus.htm

Turkey Point

This is a swinging beach town for the younger set. There is one main road that runs parallel to kilometres of white sand beach that is usually packed every hot summer weekend; only cottagers or locals who live here year-round use the little side roads. The main focal point for evening entertainment (again, for the younger set) is the **Turkey Point Hotel**, with live bands and a large outdoor patio conveniently located along the town's only main road.

Turkey Point is a good, busy spot to take a break from your drive, work on your suntan and swim in a lake so wide it resembles an ocean. This is a terrific little beach resort if you want to rent a cottage on the lake and get away from it all.

Tel: (519) 426-3288. www.norfolktourism.ca

Kernal Peanuts

When approaching Turkey Point along Highway 24, jog north off the highway towards the village of Vittoria to stop at Kernal Peanuts for fresh-roasted peanuts, candies, fudge, peanut butter (of course) and Kernal's own addictive almond butter spread. For many years the area's main industry was tobacco. However, the crops have been cut back by government regulations and now many farmers have switched over to such crops as peanuts and ginseng. This farm, owned and operated by Ernie and Nancy Ratz, was one of the first to plant peanuts and they have been refining their crops for more than 30 years to become the largest peanut farm in the country. Guided tours of the 'peanut patch' are available as well as the aromatic plant where you can watch the shelling, roasting and mixing of real peanut butter.

RR1. Vittoria. Tel: (519) 426-9222.
www.canadianpeanuts.com

Port Dover

Unlike the previous two locations, this town has every amenity – grocery and video stores, bars and restaurants, hotels and inns, summer theatre and a nautical museum. Port Dover is the quintessential beach town, with fishing tugs, yachts and sailing boats highlighted by one of the most picturesque lighthouse piers anywhere on the lake.

Port Dover formerly held the title of 'largest freshwater fishing port in the world', but, alas, the size of the catch has diminished in the past few decades.

However, there is still enough to satisfy the hordes of hungry summer visitors who chow down on big platters of perch in every restaurant in town – specifically the Erie Beach, Knechtel's and The Fisherman's Catch.

There seems to be an unofficial rule that every eating establishment must serve perch.

One exception is Imaginations Fine Foods – a blend of deli, grocery and 'big-city' fine-food shop in a little beach town. Many locals, who need a change from perch every day, visit this shop for one of chef Anthony's huge deli sandwiches or flash-frozen pre-cooked entrées.

Dover is becoming known for its 'theme weekends' such as 'Fish Fest' in July and 'Art & Crafts in the Park' in August. The town also plays host to a 'happening' every Friday the 13th – whenever it falls in the calendar year. Some 100,000 motorcycle enthusiasts arrive in this little town of 6,000 for a day-long party.

Tourist attractions include the **Lighthouse Theatre**, which presents professional summer stock, and the **Port Dover Harbour Museum** at the bottom of Harbor Street (drive straight down Main which ends at the harbour) with its nautical treasures including some artefacts from the *Titanic*. If you want to see 'the hidden Dover', take the **RiverRider**, a 40-passenger pontoon boat that sails 'up the crick' past fishing tugs, yacht clubs, million-dollar homes and nature reserves.

The Port Dover Board of Trade. 19
Market Street West. Tel: (519) 583-1314.
www.portdover.ca

Selkirk Provincial Park

The drive into this community winds along the shoreline with Lake Erie on one side and petite little cottages along the other – many of them for summer rentals. Though you will find all the small-town amenities in Selkirk, most people come to the area for the terrific park right by the lake. There are 142 camping pitches (67 with electricity) as well as two selected areas that can hold a group of 30 campers. If you do plan on camping, book your site as soon as possible through the provincial website. This is the place to stop for a picnic lunch (use one of the many barbecues in the park), some sunbathing, a swim or just to relax in a beautiful spot before you continue your drive around Ontario's South Coast.

Tel: (905) 776-2600.
www.ontarioparks.com

Port Colborne/Welland Canal

Formerly a sleepy little dormitory community for the Niagara region, Port Colborne recently woke up when a new breed of younger entrepreneur moved into the community with trendy restaurants, professional theatre (in the Showboat Theatre), arts and crafts boutiques (Folk Arts Council) and even an operatic society. This is a perfectly preserved Ontario town, outwardly frozen somewhere in the 1950s, which is just now making up for lost time with a new generation who have chosen to ply their craft, be it award-winning cuisine or unique craftwork, in a more relaxed

Welland Canal – linking Lake Erie with Lake Ontario

small-town setting just 30 minutes from the wall-to-wall tourists in Niagara Falls.

This is also the best place to explore the **Welland Canal** – an engineering marvel of the 20th century that linked Lake Ontario with Lake Erie: the only alternative route for travel through the Great Lakes was over Niagara Falls.

The canal itself is 43km (27 miles) long and has eight locks; it takes about ten hours to pass through the system. The height distance between the two lakes is 100m (328ft). The Clarence Street bridge, in Port Colborne, is one of the few operating 'lift' bridges remaining in the province.

66 Charlotte Street, Port Colborne.
Tel: (905) 835-2900.
www.city.portcolborne.on.ca

'Harbour hopping'

Since much of Canada freezes up for six months of the year, local sailors take full advantage of the warm springs and hot humid summers of Ontario.

Many tourists rent houseboats for a summer holiday, cruising through the rivers and locks of the Trent-Severn and Rideau inland channels, while others take to the waters of the St Lawrence Seaway or the many lakes in Ontario. At the last count, tourism officials listed half-a-million lakes in Ontario alone.

However, one of the most popular summer getaways is cruising along Ontario's shoreline of Lake Huron and/or Lake Erie.

Lake Huron

Lake Huron

If you count the beaches of its 30,000 islands, Lake Huron has the largest shoreline of the five Great Lakes. These islands – mind you, some are very tiny! – are scattered throughout the 332-km (206-mile) wide and 295-km (183-mile) long lake that has an average depth of 59m (195ft). The largest island is Manitoulin, which is the largest freshwater island in the world. Many sailors just take a week of their holiday and cruise around this huge island – stopping at all the little ports and inlets.

The attractions along the way include spectacular scuba diving at Tobermory (there are numerous shipwrecks at the underwater Fathom Five Park – which should be a warning to sailors about the unpredictability of the Great Lakes), the sandy shores of the popular Sauble Beach, and Port Elgin, Kincardine, Goderich, Bayfield, Grand Bend and Sarnia along the coast .

In the far south the lake touches the American border at Port Huron in the state of Michigan.

The yachtsman or woman can then sail down the connecting Saint Clair River into Lake St Clair, then on to the border cities of Windsor and Detroit

Lake Erie

and down the Detroit River into Lake Erie.

Lake Erie

Lake Erie was named after the Erie tribe of Iroquois Indians (the Iroquois word Erielhonan means 'long tail of a cougar'). The lake is the 12th-largest freshwater lake in the world and the second smallest of the five Great Lakes; it is also the shallowest, with an average depth of only 19m (62ft), making it the warmest water in which to swim. Boaters can cruise between Amherstburg (just south of Windsor) and historic Fort Erie (near Niagara Falls). (*For detailed information of the ports along the Lake Erie shoreline, see the South Coast on pp60–65.*)

Boat rentals

Sailors without their own boats or yachts can find rental agencies in the Lake Huron ports of Kincardine, Goderich and Grand Bend or closer to Lake Erie in the city of Windsor or Amherstburg. (*For full information on ports and rentals: www.stepashore.com.*)

Lake safety

The waters are patrolled by both the Ontario Provincial Police (OPP) water safety division and Canadian Coast Guard vessels. Note that an owner or renter of a boat or yacht must have a document or licence stating they have a 'proof of competency' to operate a vessel. Licences from other jurisdictions (United States, Britain, etc.) are also accepted. Check the official government site for details (*www.boatingsafety.gc.ca*).

This is a wonderfully relaxing way to explore the sandy beaches, fishing villages and friendly shoreline of Ontario – and the best method for working on your summer tan. But remember, make sure you have your lifejackets, charts and maps with you. And a VHF radio and GPS guidance system can only add to your safety on the waters.

Kingston and environs

Known as 'The Limestone City' – created from the rocks of local limestone quarries – Kingston is blessed with spectacular architecture, a natural scenic harbour, and a year-round moderate climate thanks to its shoreline location at the entrance of the St Lawrence Seaway. In fact, the location is so good that early founders chose this site as the first capital of 'the United Canadas' in 1841.

Kingston prospered as a naval and military base and became the leading commercial centre between Montréal and Lake Superior. For all its big-city amenities (population 155,000), Kingston has the accessibility of a small town with the added bonus of rural farm life on one side and a watery playground on the other.
Tourism Kingston. 209 Ontario Street.

Tel: (613) 548-4415.
www.kingstoncanada.com

Confederation Tour Trolley

This tour is the best, brief (one-hour) overview a visitor will receive on Kingston and its colourful history. The Confederation Trolley ride includes highlights such the Royal Military College, Fort Henry, Fort Frontenac, the

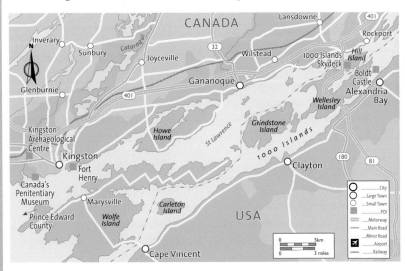

city's penitentiary, Queen's University and even Bellevue House, the residence of Sir John A Macdonald, the country's first prime minister.

290 Ontario Street. Tel: (613) 548-4453. Email: trolley@kingstonchamber.on.ca

Fort Henry

Constructed during the War of 1812, Fort Henry was built to repel those uncivilised invaders from the United States as they waged war against Great Britain. The area was seen as especially vulnerable due to its close proximity to the US border just a few kilometres across the St. Lawrence River. Building the fort must have scared away the invaders because there were never any attempts to storm the gates. Today the fort is open for daily public inspection between May and September and staffed by guides (mostly students from the Royal Military College) wearing the period costumes and muskets of the British army. The most impressive historical routine is the Sunset Ceremony held every Wednesday throughout the summer when the 'soldiers' perform with all the pomp and pageantry of an 1867 British drill team; the drum beats of the military tattoo accompany the precision of drill and firing manoeuvres, followed by fireworks over the battlement walls.

LaSalle Causeway (off Highway 2). Tel: (613) 542-7388. www.forthenry.com. Open: May–Oct daily 10am–5pm. Admission charge.

Kingston Archaeological Centre

This local museum presents the history of the area from the first native tribes, going back to approximately 8000 BC, up to the late 19th century. The Cataraqui Archaeological Research Foundation (named after an Iroquois word for the area, meaning 'impregnable' or 'place of retreat') has gathered together artefacts of stone and bone to represent the first settlers to Kingston, as well as many items from the early 17th-century days of the French explorers and fur trappers. Few cities in North America have such a comprehensive museum dedicated to its past.

72 Gilmore Avenue. Tel: (613) 542-3483. www.carf.info. Open: Tue–Sun 10am–5pm. Closed: Mon. Admission charge.

Marine Museum of the Great Lakes

The Marine Museum pays homage to the history of shipping and navigation through the Great Lakes system from the early days of native war canoes and French fur trappers to the massive lake freighters and pleasure yachts of today. The Interpretation Centre helps relate the history with a multimedia theatre, while walking below the huge ship *Alexander Henry*, at the bottom of its dry dock, will emphasise the skills and complexities of ship construction.

55 Ontario Street. Tel: (613) 542-2261. www.marmuseum.ca. Open: daily in summer 10am–5pm (until noon Sun). Admission charge.

Canada's Penitentiary Museum

Kingston is known throughout the country for Queen's University. However, when most Canadians hear the word Kingston, they still think of 'the Pen' – the federal penitentiary located in this city. Tours are not available, of course, but the city wisely opened a museum to educate the public in the works of Corrections Canada and the legal system of 'crime and punishment' in Canada – from hard labour to education and counselling. Collectors will want to visit and pick up copies of early badges worn by prison guards – such as the rare Victorian 'Shako Plato' star-shaped badge issued to officials in 1867 when Canada officially became a nation.

55 King Street West. Tel: (613) 530-3122.

Boldt Castle is located on Heart Island in the 1000 Islands

www.penitentiarymuseum.ca. Open: daily 10am–4pm. Donations accepted.

KINGSTON ENVIRONS
Wolfe Island

The western coast of this little island juts out into Lake Ontario while the other shores all belong to the St Lawrence Seaway. The island, only a few minutes' ferry ride from the harbour in Kingston, is the same distance from Cape Vincent, New York State, on the other side of the river. Wolfe Island is about 30km (19 miles) long and ranges anywhere from 2km to 12km (1 mile to 7 miles) in width. When residents of Kingston want to escape their urban existence, they often spend a quiet weekend fishing, swimming, sailing, bird-watching, cycling or cross-country skiing in the winter on their 'private' island domain. Wolfe Island, named after British General James Wolfe, was originally called Ganounkouenot, meaning 'long island standing up'.
Wolfe Island Business and Tourism Association. Tel: (613) 385-1875.
www.wolfeisland.com

1000 Islands

Gananoque is a pretty little Ontario town about 30km (19 miles) east of Kingston along the St Lawrence. However, most people come here just to leave right away; this is where all the tour boats depart for cruises through the spectacular 1000 Islands. Actually there are a total of 1,864 islands – though some may seem like little blips of land in the Seaway. (The definition of an island in the St Lawrence is that it must be above water 365 days of the year and has to support at least two living trees.) Each little island is unique, with its own mixture of granite cliffs, sandy bays, dark pines and colourful maple trees – a late September cruise is spectacularly beautiful with the changing autumn foliage. There are only four islands that can be reached by either ferry service or fixed bridge – Wolfe, Wellesley, Hill and Howe.

Boldt Castle

Whatever cruise line you choose, make sure that it stops for an exploration of Boldt Castle on Heart Island. This is a huge, crumbling 120-room Rhineland-style castle and yacht house built at the beginning of the 20th century. Note, however, that Boldt Castle is located in US waters. Passengers arriving from Canadian ports must provide proper identification to US Customs before they can leave the ship.
1000 Island Tourism.
Tel: (800) 8-ISLAND.
www.1000islandsgananoque.com

The following is a selection of cruise companies that include Boldt Castle on their tours.
Gananoque Boat Lines *10 Water Street, Gananoque. Tel: (613) 382-2144.*
www.ganboatline.com
Heritage 1000 Islands Cruises
Rockport. Tel: (613) 659-3151.
www.1000islandscruises.com

Rockport Boat Line *Rockport.*
Tel: (613) 659-3402.
www.rockportcruises.com

1000 Islands Skydeck
Located on Hill Island, right in the middle of the St Lawrence, the 1000 Islands Skydeck provides an awesome 360-degree view of the islands in the Seaway from a dizzying height of 130m (400ft). The glass lift whisks you up at 3m (10ft) per second to three observations decks – one is enclosed for those windy days. On a clear afternoon you can see some 65km (40 miles) along the river. You can reach Hill Island from both the Canadian and US sides of the border.
Tel: (613) 659-2335.
www.1000islandsskydeck.com.
Open: May–Oct daily 10am–7pm.
Admission charge.

Ontario Waterways (and Rideau Canal)

Many Canadians, as well as visitors, love to spend their summer on the water. Kingston is the start – or end,

Rideau Canal

depending on your route – of a 700-km (435-mile) inland waterway system through the province. The interconnecting system includes the Trent-Severn Waterway, the Bay of Quinte and the Rideau Canal between Kingston and Ottawa. The proper way to experience the waterway, however, is on a houseboat as you cruise through lakes and rivers, man-made canals and engineered locks. This is a leisurely pleasure cruise with picnic areas along the banks, sandy beaches and small town marinas. And any place you want to stop for the night is fine – just anchor your boat or tie up to a tree along the shore. For those who want to leave the 'driving' to someone else, you can get a taste of the system with a five-day voyage aboard the 45-passenger *Kawartha Voyageur* riverboat out of Kingston harbour. The National Historic Site of the Rideau Canal celebrats its 175th anniversary during the 2007 boating season.
www.rideau175.org
Kawartha Voyageur *Kingston Harbour. Tel: (800) 561-5767.*
www.ontariowaterwaycruises.com
R&R Houseboats *Bridgenorth. Tel: (705) 743-8113.*
www.rrhouseboats.com

Prince Edward County

This quiet little almost-island county (bridge, ferry or boat) just south of Kingston has become an enclave for artists, antiques collectors, sailors and city-dwellers seeking a quiet weekend retreat as an alternative to the high prices of the popular Muskokas. As a result, some of the 'big city' amenities have set up shop in the county – fine dining, trendy boutiques and art galleries. It's not enough to change the tone of this predominantly rural lifestyle but just enough to offer a choice for the new residents. The uninitiated will be forgiven if they believe they have suddenly been whisked to New England when they drive (slowly) through the village of Bloomfield, with its maritime design and friendly small-town manners, or the slightly larger Picton, with old-world country style and a main street that leads right to the water's edge.

What to do in Prince Edward County? First of all, relax. Most people start this at the **Sandbanks Provincial Park** – which is just as it sounds, a massive mountain of sand that runs for miles along the shores of Lake Ontario. This park is just as popular with adults as it is with children. Camping is at a premium: book your site early.

The latest draw to the county is the **Taste Trail**, culinary and wine experiences (*www.tastetrail.ca*) that include local wineries (Sandbanks Estate and Closson Chase), farm tours, fresh produce markets and culinary creations using only county-produced ingredients.
116 Main Street. Tel: (613) 476-2421. www.pec.on.ca

Ottawa

Ottawa has long held the reputation of being one of the most beautiful capital cities in the world – especially during spring when thousands, perhaps millions, of dazzling tulips burst forth all over the city. The city, along with its Québec neighbours across the river in Gatineau (formerly known as Hull) combines as one to become Canada's Capital Region. Ottawa city contains all the requisite government buildings found in any capital city, as well as 29 museums and galleries, yet remains very accessible and retains the friendly feel of a small town; you can park your car and walk anywhere in Ottawa.

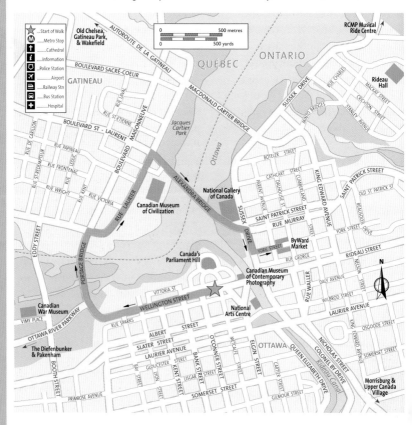

The American border is only one hour away, the weekend resorts and ski hills are within half an hour's drive, and the city also boasts the longest ice-skating rink in the world.
Ottawa Tourism. 130 Albert Street, Ottawa. Tel: (613) 237-6822.
www.ottawatourism.ca

Canada's Parliament Hill

The three huge buildings that house the federal government of Canada, and play home to its nationally elected politicians, sit atop a gorgeous hillside setting overlooking the Ottawa River with a backdrop of the City of Gatineau. These huge neo-Gothic buildings of granite and stone (with copper-covered roofs) were built between 1859 and 1866, and recently received a four-year facelift that has restored them to former 19th-century glory. The Centre Block is the main building that features the House of Commons, the seat of federal government, while the East and West Blocks respectively contain offices of the politicians and government staff. There is a Visitors' Gallery in the House of Commons. The view from high, from the observation level of the Peace Tower, is spectacular.

To witness a stirring spectacle of pomp and ceremony get to the Hill before 10am any morning from June to August for the colourful military drill and music of the **Changing of the Guard**.
Wellington Street. Tel: (613) 996-0896.
www.parl.gc.ca

Sound and Light Show

From July to September, Parliament Hill features a free, half-hour Sound and Light Show that highlights breathtaking Canadian landscapes – massive images are carved in light on the parliament buildings – with a bilingual narration describing the creation of the country.
Tel: (613) 233-1126.
www.canadascapital.gc.ca

Canadian Museum of Civilization

Located on the Québec side of the river, this amazing structure is itself a work of art; the building is all curves, designed to imitate the flow of Canadian winds and waters. Métis (First Nation) architect Douglas Cardinal created the museum as a visual representation of the geological formation of the country

Old tank in the Canadian War Museum

through the elements of nature. The interior is a fascinating collection of artefacts that display the Canadian story from the early legends of the country's First Nations to the exploration of the original French *voyageurs*. In addition, the museum houses both the Canadian Children's Museum (one of the largest in the world) and the Canadian Postal Museum.

One tip: do not miss whatever is showing in the combined IMAX/ OMNIMAX theatre – this is the closest you will come to soaring without leaving the ground.
100 Laurier Street, Gatineau. Tel: (819) 776-7000. www.civilization.ca. Open: May–Sept daily 9am–6pm. Admission charge.

Canadian Museum of Contemporary Photography

As part of the National Museum of Canada, this homage to the photographic image is housed in a reconstructed railway tunnel right beside the first locks of the Rideau Canal. The museum's permanent gallery showcases 160,000 photographs that highlight not only the Canadian scene but also images from around the world as captured through the lens of the camera.
1 Rideau Canal. Tel: (613) 990-8257. www.cmcp.gallery.ca. Open: May–Sept daily 9am–6pm. Admission charge.

Canadian War Museum

The museum opened on 8 May 2005 to commemorate the 60-year anniversary of the end of World War II in Europe. It traces the history of military involvement in Canada from the early days of exploration by New France and the defence mounted to repel the American invaders in the War of 1812, to the sacrifice of Canadian soldiers in the wars of the 20th century and the country's role today as part of the UN peacekeeping forces around the world.
1 Vimy Place. Tel: (613) 776-8600. www.warmuseum.ca. Open: May–Sept daily 9am–6pm. Admission charge.

Confederation Boulevard
See Walk, p80.

The Diefenbunker

This Cold War curiosity conjures up the fear and paranoia of the 1950s and early 1960s when all children in Canada received classroom training in the event of a nuclear attack. This massive bomb shelter, named after John Diefenbaker (the Canadian prime minister of the day), is a deeply buried, four-storey, 9,300sq m (100,000sq ft) underground bunker designed to withstand a nuclear attack. It was built to protect members of the government and the military.
3911 Carp Road. Tel: (613) 839-0007. www.diefenbunker.ca. Daily tours in English and French in July and Aug from 10am. Limited tours during winter season. Admission charge.

National Arts Centre

Home to the NAC Orchestra, this is the National Capital Region's

pre-eminent centre for the performing arts, designed as a diverse showcase to highlight the best of world theatre, dance, music and variety acts. The theatre's mandate is to present an annual programme of bilingual entertainment, French and English, with an occasional bilingual production such as Michel Tremblay's *Balconville*. The theatre plays host to troupes from all over the world – many of whom are introducing their country's artistic achievements for the first time in Canada.
55 Elgin Street. Tel: (613) 833-3059.
www.nac-cna.ca

National Gallery of Canada

This gallery is a must-see for anyone interested in – or simply curious about – Canadian and Inuit works of art. The permanent collection features sketch

National Gallery of Canada

works from the first settlers to the modern works of Robert Bateman. And, naturally, the Group of Seven (*see p35*). The art and craft of Canada's First Nations are prominently displayed through drawings and sculpture that capture the centuries-old legends of gods and creation.
380 Sussex Drive. Tel: (613) 990-1985.
www.national.gallery.ca. Open: daily 10am–5pm. Admission charge.

Ottawa's ByWard Market

This trendy enclave in the middle of town, just a few minutes' walk from Parliament Hill, is a bustling area of cool bars, cafés and restaurants all surrounding a huge town square that is the scene of a thriving farmers' market. The original market was designed in 1826 (by Lt Col John By, architect of the Rideau Canal) as a large, open area where farmers could display their wares. The market has always remained a daily feature of Ottawa life; merchants set up both indoors and on the street to display just-picked farm vegetables, prime cuts of beef or speciality cheeses.
55 ByWard Market Square.
Tel: (613) 244-4410.
www.bywardmarket@ottawa.ca

RCMP Musical Ride Centre

For many, this is the reason to visit Canada: the famed Royal Canadian Mounted Police Musical Ride – an intricate and flashy cavalry drill choreographed to music featuring 32 riders and their magnificent steeds. The

Ottawa's annual Winterlude festival

RCMP Musical Ride takes place during the Mounties' Sunset Ceremonies and unfortunately is rarely performed anymore. The long-standing tradition takes place only in the Nation's Capital between 28 June and 2 July, the weekend that Canada celebrates its 1 July founding. For those who can't attend the ceremony itself, there is an **RCMP Musical Ride Centre** where visitors can tour the stables and learn the history of the RCMP.
1 Sandridge Road. Tel: (613) 998-8199. www.rcmp-grc.gc.ca

Rideau Canal

One of the most popular summer vacations in Ontario is to rent a fully stocked houseboat for a cruise along the Rideau Canal. The canal meanders 200km (124 miles) from Kingston to Ottawa – through beautiful lakes, rivers and canals – right up to the staircase of eight locks literally at the base of Parliament Hill. Today a tourist delight, it was originally conceived as a supply route between the Ottawa River and Lake Ontario following the War of 1812. It took six years for thousands of stonemasons and labourers to carve the canal through the unexplored wilds of eastern Ontario. The canal, supervised by Colonel John By of the British Royal Engineers, has been hailed as one of the greatest engineering feats of the 19th century. There are museums at the lock stations and countless picnic, barbecue and camping facilities en route. The city banks of the Rideau are always filled with thousands of civil servants enjoying a lunchtime picnic or afternoon break.

Rideau Canal National Historic Site of Canada. Tel: (613) 283-5170.
www.pc.gc.ca

Rideau Hall

This is the official residence of the governor general, the Queen's representative in Canada, a stately manor built on a beautiful 35-ha (87-acre) estate. Although there are no scheduled tours of the estate, indoor tours can be arranged for groups. However, the general public is free to wander outdoors through the Canadian Heritage Gardens which feature 92 varieties of roses symbolising the country's cultural mosaic. The public can also make use of the estate's huge skating rink during the icy months of winter. Everyone is invited to attend the governor general's New Year's Levée on New Year's Day, as well as a June Garden Party that has a flexible date. There is a visitors' information booth on site.

1 Sussex Drive.
Tel: (613) 991-4422. www.gg.ca.
Open: daily 8am–sunset.
Free admission.

OTTAWA ENVIRONS
Fulton's Pancake House and Sugar Bush

The indigenous maple syrup is probably the most recognisable of all Canadian food products – and much more popular than moose burgers or beaver tails. This 162-ha (400-acre) site is the perfect spot to explore all things mapley. And not just the syrup, but also maple sugar candy, maple syrup-covered peanuts – the list is endless. The tour of the property includes a look at the maple syrup process – from sap to jar – and if you visit in early spring, you will be able to help 'tap' the trees. Winter activities include cross-country skiing, snowshoeing, dog sledding, sleigh rides and an old-fashioned, somewhat messy taffy pull (stretching-out long strands of candy).

291, 6th Concession Road, Pakenham.
Tel: (613) 256-3867.
www.fultons.on.ca

RIDEAU CANAL SKATEWAY

It gets cold in Ottawa during those long winter months and most residents feel that, if you can't escape it, you might as well enjoy it. Since the Rideau Canal winds right through the centre of Ottawa, the city fathers have turned the waterway into the world's longest skating rink, as designated by Guinness World Records. At 7.8km (4.8 miles), with an ice surface equal to 90 Olympic-sized rinks, the frozen canal plays host to some 750,000 ice skaters each season. For safety reasons, the official season lasts only 64 days – so plan your visit during January and February for maximum skating pleasure.

Many of the people who live in homes along the Rideau skate into work every day.

The Skateway is the centre of activities every February when Ottawa celebrates **Winterlude** with snow and ice sculpture creations all over the city, skating competitions on the Rideau and cross-country skiing in the Gatineaus. There are numerous refreshment booths serving hot mulled cider.

Walk: Confederation Boulevard

The nation's capital, a combination of the Ontario city of Ottawa and the Québec City of Gatineau, is one of the most walkable cities in the country. This walk in two provinces will provide you with the political and historical highlights, while ending the day with a relaxing dinner in modern 21st-century style.

Allow a full day. See map on p74 for route.

As you walk out of your downtown hotel all of Ottawa is laid out before you – there are the Parliament Buildings in front of you, and the National Gallery behind you, which is beside the National Mint and right across from the ByWard Market. Park your car and pick up your map of the city's Confederation Boulevard.

Where to start? Parliament Hill (*see p75*), of course, on Wellington Street. This is the centre of Canada's government where all the elected federal Members of Parliament congregate to bicker and quarrel and cause citizens to wonder if democracy is truly the best form of government. For a look at the people running the country, feel free to drop into Parliament's Visitors' Gallery and watch the political free-for-all.

Best to ignore the politicians and take the lift to the observation deck of the Hill's Centre Block for an aerial view of the lovely Gatineau scenery across the Ottawa River – the brilliant colours of late September create the most spectacular view.

Continue west on Wellington, past the Confederation and Justice buildings, and follow the street across Portage Bridge (just past the Library and Archives building) over the Ottawa River and into the Province of Québec.

This now becomes Laurier Avenue as soon as you get off the bridge. Turn right (east) and follow the street a few blocks to the stunning Canadian Museum of Civilization (*see p75*), which traces Canada's development from the Vikings to the present day with an eclectic combination of archaeology and history, as well as folklore and ethnic contributions.

Whenever you can drag yourself away (you could spend a few days in this museum), walk a little further east and perhaps enjoy a picnic lunch in Jacques Cartier Park or drop into the restaurant in the adjacent marina.

Then walk back into Ontario across

the Alexandra Bridge where you will be greeted by a statue of Champlain in the lovely little Nepean Point parklands. Continue your stroll, and one block later you will bump into the National Gallery of Canada (*see p77*) where all the national treasures of art and literature of Canada's history are fully displayed. (Note: The United States embassy is just outside the museum doors of Sussex Street.)

After a day of politics, history and culture, treat yourself to a late-afternoon libation or dinner at one of the many bars and restaurants in the trendy, fun, yet historic market area just across Sussex Drive into Ottawa's ByWard Market (*see p77*).

Looking over the Ottowa River

Gatineau Park

This is one of the most popular getaways for anyone living in the National Capital Region – a scenic and welcoming park area just 15 minutes across the river from Parliament Hill. The Gatineau was created by glaciers 10,000 years ago and provided a home for Canada's people for some 5,000 years. There are manicured trails for hiking, biking and cross-country skiing throughout the 363-sq km (139-sq mile) park, as well as picnic areas, camping and beach sites for swimming. Bird-watchers can while away their days looking for all 230 species of birds (including the rare pileated woodpecker), and hikers heading deeper into the woods will probably see white-tailed deer, as well as beavers building their dams. Campers may huddle closer to the fire when a timber wolf or two howls somewhere in the night.

Highway # 5 North, Chelsea.
Tel: (819) 827-2020.
www.canadascapital.gc.ca/gatineau

Mackenzie King Estate

Located in the Gatineau Park, this house was designed by William Lyon Mackenzie King, the tenth prime minister of Canada and one of the first leaders to realise the importance of the preservation and conservation of the natural world around us. King bequeathed his home and 231-ha (570-acre) estate to the nation with the proviso that it would forever remain a public park. The mansion was restored to its original splendour and the public can now witness the lifestyle of a former leader of Canada on daily tours. Apparently Mackenzie King, a lifelong bachelor, kept in contact with his dead mother through a medium!

33 Scott Road, Chelsea.
Tel: (819) 827-2020.
www.canadascapital.gc.ca/gatineau.
Open: May–Oct daily 11am–5pm.
Free admission.

Upper Canada Village

An easy hour's drive south of Ottawa will transport you into a time warp circa 1860 when you enter the gates of Upper Canada Village. This village was re-created in 1959 when many early settlements had to be flooded by the excavation of the St Lawrence Seaway. The buildings and artefacts are all original and authentic to the era, from the blacksmith shop and schoolhouse to the little church and bakery. The costumed characters roaming throughout the village are not that old, however, but they do remain in their 1860 roles and provide a delightful commentary about the daily workings of the village.

Morrisburg. Tel: (613) 543-3704.
www.uppercanadavillage.com.
Open: May–Sept daily 9.30am–5pm.
Admission charge.

Villages of Wakefield and Chelsea

These two little time-warp villages, located in the Outaouais (Oo-ta-way) area just across the river from Ottawa, have become popular with locals as well as visitors. Both towns have an immediate historic feel (you almost think you are on a film set) and these are villages for which the over-used word 'quaint' truly does apply. The tiny towns feature boutiques, cafés, old-style bakeries and heritage attractions. To help transport you back a century or two, get on board the little Hull-Chelsea-Wakefield Steam Train, the last authentic steam-powered locomotive in eastern Canada, which will whisk you into the past and bring you back later that same day.

HCW Steam Train *165 rue Deveault, Gatineau. Tel: (819) 778-7246. www.steamtrain.ca*

Whitewater rafting

One of the major rites of summer in the province is the challenge of facing the raging white waters of the Ottawa River on a wildly bucking inflatable raft. Go figure! The object is to put about 12 people in a rubber raft, gently paddle along the calm waters, then watch their faces as the guide turns a bend and you start rushing toward a 3-m (10-ft) waterfall. This is one of the great thrill rides of summer! This can be a great day trip, with a shore lunch along the way, but most people spend the weekend at the official campsite, sitting around the campfire at night, reliving the excitement of the raging rapids, and ready to face the great watery unknown the next day. Oh yes, and you will get very, very wet.

Whitewater rafting companies.
Foresters Falls:
OWL Rafting. *Tel: (613) 238-7238. www.owlrafting.com*
Wilderness Tours. *Tel: (613) 646-2291. www.wildernesstours.com. Daily from Apr–Oct. Prices vary, call for details.*

The Hull-Chelsea-Wakefield Steam Train

Montréal

Joie de vivre. Joy of life. This is one of the first phrases you will learn in La Belle Province. You will be able to feel it everywhere you go – on the streets, in the restaurants and most certainly in the crowded pubs and pavement cafés.

Sure, the Anglo city of Toronto is bigger, but who cares? Not the Montréalers because they are having too much fun. In this city it is impolite to ask someone 'What do you do?' (i.e. your profession). Instead, Montréalers ask, 'What do you do for fun?'

Joie de vivre. Just ask the revellers out every night of the week in the artists' enclave of Plateau Mont-Royal, the vibrant student Quartier Latin, the packed restaurants and discos of Crescent Street or standing in line waiting to enter the laid-back

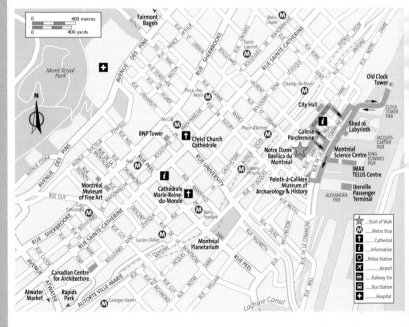

lounges and deli delights of
The Main.
Tourism Montréal. 1555 rue Peel.
Tel: (514) 844-3264.
www.tourism.montreal.org

Canadian Centre for Architecture
This international research centre and
museum has always been recognised for
its historical collections and quality of
its touring exhibitions – and the design
of the building itself has won various
international awards. There are guided
tours available through this history
of architectural achievement
(specifically Canadian design) and the
public is also invited to explore the
Shaughnessy House, one of the only
19th-century Montréal houses open
for display.
1920 rue Baile. Tel: (514) 939-7026.
www.cca.qc.ca. Open: Wed–Sun
10am–5pm. Closed: Mon and Tue.
Admission charge.

Crescent Street
Chic and trendy. Just north of the main
de Maisonneuve Boulevard in the
middle of the city, locals and tourists
all head to this area, which is packed
with luxury boutiques and designer
showrooms as well as popular
nightclubs, restaurants, bars and
street-side cafés all enveloped in a
touch of class by the street's elegant
Victorian architecture. This lively
area is known for its fun and
festivity until the wee hours of
the morning.

Montréal viewed from Mont Royal

Fairmount Bagel Bakery
There are certain items or attractions
that make a city unique – in Montréal
one of those items is bagels, bagels and
more bagels (any Montréaler will tell
you this is one of the major food
groups). The first thing you notice
when approaching this shop is that
there is no lock on the front door –
that's because they work 24 hours a day,
seven days a week. Locals drop in at any
and every hour of the day or night for
piping-hot fresh bagels right out of the
wood-burning ovens (each bagel is
made individually by hand). Customers
can watch as a massive countertop of
dough – perhaps 3m (10ft) long and
1m (3ft) high – is kneaded and sliced
and formed into perfect rings ready for
the baking pan. Though Fairmont will
never reveal its 77-year-old Jewish
European secret recipe for these warm
and chewy culinary staples, it does
involve just a *soupçon* of honey (or is
that maple syrup?) in the mix.
74 rue Fairmont Ouest at Urbain.
Tel: (514) 272-0667. Open: always!

Walk: Vieux Montréal and Vieux-Port

A walk through Old Montréal is an eclectic blend of 18th-century art, culture and history mixed with the technology of the 21st-century. The following is merely a sample of some of the highlights you will discover along the way.

Allow a whole day. See map on p84 for route.

Start your stroll at the awesome **Notre Dame Basilica du Montréal** (100 rue Notre Dame et rue Saint-Sulpice), a masterwork of Gothic Revival architecture with a stunning interior of sculpted wood and gold leaf. You can return in the evening for the 'sound and light' illuminations depicting the founding of the city.

Continue along rue Le Royer, right behind the basilica, for some terrific window-shopping (and buying, of course) in the traditional shops and boutiques along the **Hôtel-Dieu**. At the end of the street, turn right along boulevard Saint-Laurent and continue shopping on **Saint-Paul** et **de la Commune** street. Check out the **Galerie Parchemine** at 40 rue Saint Paul; you can not only purchase some original Québec art and sculpture but also antique frames from France.

If you can tear yourself away from this wonderful selection of

Notre-Dame's ornate interior

consumerism, turn north on place Jacques Cartier and walk a few blocks to **City Hall** at 275 rue Notre Dame. Built between 1872 and 1878, this is a truly impressive structure for local government (tours are available during the day).

Next, turn south along Saint-Claude and into the **Vieux-Port** and to the **Old Clock Tower** at the furthest eastern tip of the port along the appropriately named Clock Tower Pier. The tower is a memorial to the merchant fleet who lost their lives during World War I. You can climb the tower for a view of the Old Port.

Retrace your steps to the 2.5-km (1^1/$_2$-mile) long boardwalk that will take you through the parks, past cruise ships, impromptu concerts, jugglers and clowns along the **Vieux-Port (Old Port) of Montréal**. Along the way, stop at **Shed 16 Labyrinth** (Jacques Cartier Pier) for a journey through atmospheric mazes and mysterious paths in this funhouse converted from an old waterfront shed.

Continuing west, you will discover the delights of science, technology and interactive media at the **Montréal Science Centre**, with adjoining **IMAX TELUS Centre** on the King Edward Pier right at the corner of boulevard Saint-Laurent et de la Commune.

It is at this point that you reach the **Iberville Passenger Terminal**, where thousands of cruise ships dock annually at Pier Alexandra. This is also the pier where the visitor can book cruises

The illuminated City Hall

along the St Lawrence River and its tributaries.

Return to the past with a visit to the **Pointe-à-Callière Museum of Archaeology and History**. This 'living museum', a national historic site, is built on the site of the first settlement of Montréal and features a multimedia presentation of the explorers who braved an unknown ocean voyage to discover this New World. It is a perfect summation of your tour as you wander (make that 'wonder') through the centuries.

At this point, you will have had a busy day. Time to treat yourself to a snack of 'steak frites' and a drink at any of the many portside restaurants.

Montréal's islands/Parc Jean-Drapeau

You can drive, bike or take a ferry to the islands of Île Sainte-Hélène and Île Notre-Dame from the Old Port of Montréal. These formerly deserted little islands were developed for Montréal's Expo '67 (commuters only drove across them on the way to work) and have since become incredibly popular with Montréalers. Much of the land has been turned into the well-manicured Parc Jean-Drapeau (named after the former mayor who brought Expo to the city), which features ice skating and cross-country skiing in the winter, swimming and fishing in the summer. There is also a major casino/entertainment complex, a biodome of Canadian environment, a family amusement park and the world-famous Habitat '67 all within a few minutes from the shores of the city.

Casino Montréal

Seen at night, this brightly lit grand structure on the little island of Notre-Dame reflects shimmering light across the water, sending out its message to 'come and play'. And there is plenty of space to play in: 120 gaming tables (blackjack, roulette, baccarat, etc) and more than 3,000 slot machines. However, there is much more to Casino Montréal than the thrill of watching your money disappear at the craps table. This complex features four first-class restaurants, four distinctive lounges, a permanent Las Vegas-style cabaret show and touring musical acts and world-renowned singers.

Many guests visit Casino Montréal for an evening out and never experience a game of chance.

1 avenue du Casino. Île Notre-Dame. Bus 167. Tel: (515) 392-0909. www.casinos-quebec.com

Casino Montréal

Habitat '67

Forty years after it was first constructed, this building-block patchwork of housing units remains a striking sight. Designed for the 1967 World Exhibition by Moshe Safdie on this reclaimed spit of land in the St Lawrence, Habitat '67 is an avant-garde style by anyone's standards. There is a constant waiting list for this jigsaw puzzle of apartments and the complex is still one of the most photographed pieces of practical art in the city.

Environment Canada's Biosphère

This amazing geodesic dome, which housed the United States pavilion during Expo '67, was designed by architectural genius Buckminster Fuller. The structure has now become a biosphere dedicated to Canada's environmental system – specifically the ecosystem of the St Lawrence Seaway and connecting Great Lakes. Visitors can wander freely among the thematic and interpretive presentations or sign up for a guided tour.
160 rue Tour-de-l'Isle, Île Sainte-Hélène. Tel: (514) 283-5000. www.biosphere.ec.gc.ca. Open: June–Sept daily 10am–6pm (closed: Tue, Sat & Sun in winter). Admission charge.

Environment Canada's Biosphère

La Ronde

This Six Flags-operated amusement park provides great family entertainment with more than 40 rides, slides and attractions. There are also indoor and outdoor stages for entertainment and bandstands for musical acts. This is also where you'll get the best seats during the annual Montréal International Fireworks Festival.
Île Sainte-Hélène. Tel: (514) 397-2000. www.laronde.com. Open: May–Oct daily 10am–10pm. Admission charge (season pass). Two-ticket day package also available.

Montréal Museum of Fine Art

This museum, one of the first of its kind to gather together not just Canadian but universal art treasures, has become one of the most important art institutions in North America. Its permanent collection contains all types of art from antiquity (cave drawings) to modern (David Hockney) and leads the visitor through the history and development of art styles through the ages of humankind. The newly renovated galleries showcase the collection from the Renaissance up to 21st-century ultra-modern decorative trends.

1379–1380 rue Sherbroke Ouest.

The Illuminated Crowd in Montréal

Tel: (514) 285-2000. www.mmfa.qc.ca. Open: Tue–Sun 11am–5pm. Closed: Mon. Admission charge.

Montréal Planetarium

Though various cities around the world seem to have lost their planetariums (in Toronto the University initially tore down the site to make way for a condo development), Montréalers have maintained their love affair with the spectacle of a cloudless night sky projected on the expansive hemispherical dome of the Star Theatre. The state-of-the-art Zeiss equipment expands the heavens while the quiet narration pinpoints the stars and planets too far away in the solar system to be seen by the human eye. *1000 rue Saint-Jacques. Tel: (514) 872-4530. www.planetarium.montreal.qc.ca. Flexible daily schedule between 9.30am and 9.30pm; call for times. Admission charge.*

La Foule illuminée/ The Illuminated Crowd

This street-side sculpture by artist Raymond Mason has become one of the most photographed landmarks in all of Montréal. The 65 life-sized figures seems to be lit by a strong light at the front that gradually darkens on the figures towards the back rows; those at the front of the throng are eagerly looking forward, while the figures at the back turn ugly as the light becomes dim. Many passers-by only see the bright side of humankind and not the

descent into hell on the lower steps at the rear of the sculpted work.
BNP Tower – Laurentian Bank Tower. 1981 avenue McGill College.

Mont Royal Park

Officially inaugurated as a park in 1876, this protected urban greenbelt was designed by Frederick Law Olmsted, the same landscape genius who created Central Park in New York. Olmsted's trails take the hiker, biker or bird-watcher through fields and forests that make you believe you are in the Québec countryside. Cross-country skiing and ice-skating are popular throughout the winter months. This urban hillside provides a slice of country living for those who don't have the time or transportation to take them to the Laurentians or Charlevoix area.

The cross at the top of the mountain was erected in 1924. It replaced the original sign that Maisonneuve (the founder of Montréal) pounded into the grass slopes in 1664; he promised to carry a wooden cross to the summit if his young colony of settlers and soldiers survived the spring flooding along the banks of their settlement. They did. Today's cross stands 30m (98ft), and when lit at night can be seen for miles around the city.
Via Camillien-Houde Parkway (from the east) or chemin Remembrance (from the west). Tel: (514) 843-8240. www.lemontroyal.qc.ca

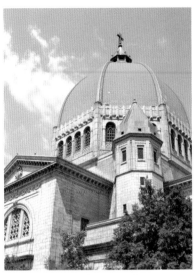
St Joseph's Oratory of Mont Royal

St Joseph's Oratory of Mont Royal
Québecers will tell you this is one of the most visited shrines in the province. The basilica on the mount boasts a huge dome of 97m (318ft) that dominates the skyline – a dome that is second in height only to St Peter's basilica in Rome. The structure itself consists of a basic chapel, a votive chapel, crypt and enough room to accommodate 10,000 worshippers for a Sunday Mass.
3800 chemin Queen Mary. Tel: (514) 733-8211. www.saint-joseph.org

Two of the most peaceful walks you will find in this city are through the two cemeteries on the mountain – **Mont Royal** and **Notre-Dame-des-Neiges**. The former, founded in 1852, comprises 59ha (145 acres) of land, gardens and terraces along the north side. Guided tours are offered, detailing the history of the city and the famous inhabitants who are buried here.

Notre-Dame-des Neiges is the country's largest Catholic cemetery and celebrates not just the lives of its inhabitants but also the cultural, historical and religious heritage of the early founders of this province.
Mont Royal Cemetery. Tel: (514) 279-7358. www.mountroyalcem.com
Notre-Dame-des-Neiges Cemetery. Tel: (514) 735-1361. www.cimetierenddn.org

Sainte-Catherine Street

Shopper alert! When people mention Montréal, most people think of Sainte-Catherine, the 15-km (9-mile) long street filled with high-end shops. This is the main east–west artery of the city, lined with major department stores, speciality boutiques, and just about any type of shop or restaurant one can imagine in a major North American city.

Underground pedestrian network

Montréal is a warm, welcoming city at any time. However, it may not feel that hospitable during those frigid months of winter. So Montréalers decided to burrow under the streets and created a vast, meandering Underground City – 33km (20 miles) of pedestrian walkways. Strollers can connect to 65 metro stops of subways and buses, as well as the central railway terminus. The clean, well-lit snowless streets are

filled with stores and boutiques (1,700), including grocery stores and delis, dry cleaners and shoe repair shops, theatres, cinemas (13), bars and restaurants (378). Many urbanites never buy a winter coat; they stroll from their apartment buildings to work or play in climate-controlled temperatures.

OLD MONTRÉAL

The fast pace of the downtown business area fades away in this historic district of 17th-century buildings, cobblestone streets and horse-drawn carriages. Relax in an old-fashioned café, a modern pub, art gallery or trendy boutique all within stone walls built to house French families some 360 years ago. (*See also Walk, p86.*)

Iberville Passenger Terminal

This is also where the traveller comes to catch a glimpse of Montréal by water. The choice of cruise ranges from a glass-domed dinner cruise (*Le Bateau-Mouche*), a three-decker party boat (*Croisières AML*), a huge catamaran-style cruise ship (*Croisières Evasion Plus*) or a whitewater excursion on the Lachine Rapids (*Sauté-Mouton*).
Iberville Passenger Terminal. Pier Alexandra. Tel: (514) 283-7011.
www.port-montreal.com
Cruise ships:
Le Bateau-Mouche. Tel: (514) 849-9952.
www.bateaumouche.ca
Croisières AML. Tel: (514) 842-9300.
www.croisieresaml.com

Croisières Evasion Plus. Tel: (514) 364-5333. www.evasionplus.com
Saute-Moutons. Tel: (514) 284-9607. www.jetboatingmontreal.com

International Flora

From June to October, acres of the Old Port are filled with a riotous rainbow of colour as 30 gardens from ecosystems around the world put down roots by the Montréal harbour. There are various sections designed to inspire gardeners who live in country homes or city condos – rooftop gardens, patio arrangements and hillside floral displays. Experts in gardening and landscape design give tours and lectures throughout the summer season.
Rue McGill, Vieux-Port. Tel: (866) 55-FLORA. www.floramontreal.ca

OLYMPIC PARK

Officially called the Hochelaga-Maisonneuve neighbourhood, the Olympic Park, about 20 minutes from the downtown core, is a day trip unto itself – perfect for kids and families, or those wishing to explore the wonders of nature while still inside an urban setting. The park itself was built for the 1976 Summer Olympics and is now a popular spot for major sporting events, rock concerts, public gatherings and afternoon picnics throughout the green parklands. The location is easy to find – just look for the massive and curvaceous **Montréal Tower** presiding over the Hochelaga-Maisonneuve area of the city. There are six swimming pools and a huge sports facility at the base of the tower, all open to the public on a daily basis. The adjacent 25-ha

Montréal

Old Montréal in the snow

(62-acre) **Maisonneuve Park** is a green space designed for sporting events including a nine-hole municipal golf course and a lighted skating rink during the non-golf season.
4141 avenue Pierre-De-Coubertin.
Tel: (514) 252-4737. www.rio.gouv.qc.ca

Montréal Biodôme

This biodome (the French word biodôme means 'house of life'), originally designed for the speed cyclists during the Montréal Olympic Games, now contains the flora and fauna of the major ecosystems of the Americas. This is a delightful journey through misty tropical forests of curious monkeys and exotic birds to the cooler climes of waddling penguins and playful seals. Each zone is designed so the visitor can get 'up close and personal' with most of the 4,800 animals – the sharks and stingrays languidly swim by the Plexiglas wall only a metre or two from your underground viewing post.
4777 avenue Pierre-De-Coubetin. Tel: (514) 868-3000. www. biodome.qc.ca. Open: June–Sept daily 9am–5pm. Admission charge.

Montréal Insectarium

A museum filled with live insects and creepy-crawly bugs. Really! And no surprise, this museum is the largest of its kind anywhere in North America. Here you'll discover the fascinating world of insects and the effect they have had on our world since the beginning of time. There are literally thousands of living and preserved insects (many countless thousands of years old, trapped inside rock and quartz formations) and collected from every corner of the Earth.
4581 rue Sherbrooke Est.
Tel: (514) 872-1400.
www.ville.montreal.qc.ca/insectarium.
Open: June–Sept daily 9am–5pm.
Admission charge.

Montréal Botanical Garden

Experts consider this to be one of the major botanical showcases in the world. Established in 1931, there are more than 22,000 species and varieties of plants on display throughout the 10 exhibition greenhouses and 30 theme gardens on this 75-ha (185-acre) site. Exotic landscapes showcase the delicate Chinese and Japanese section, while the Tree House displays the abundance of Québec's hardy verdant forests. The brilliant colours of thousands of plants create a dazzling walk among the gardens of the First Nations.
4101 rue Sherbrooke Est.
Tel: (514) 872-1400.
www.ville.montreal.qc.ca/jardin. Open: all year. Free admission.

PÔLE DES RAPIDES
Atwater Market

This vast farmers' market, with hundreds of stalls indoors and out, is packed with every type of fresh fruit, vegetable, meat, fish, fowl, baguette and speciality item you could ever imagine – if they don't have it, then very likely you really don't need it. Open seven days a week, Montréal's largest market is constantly packed with shoppers and restaurateurs, all looking for the best ingredients for that special dinner, or maybe just a bouquet of flowers from the back of someone's lorry.

The market also backs onto the Lachine Canal cycling path, so many people park their bikes and shop for dinner on the way home from work.
138 avenue Atwater. Tel: (514) 937-7754. www.marchspublics-mtl.com

Lachine Canal (NHS)

This historic waterway was instrumental in the development of both Québec and the trading fortunes of the entire country. Built in 1825 to bypass the Lachine Rapids along the St Lawrence River, the site was closed to shipping in 1970 and turned into a 14-km (9-mile) greenbelt for cyclists and strollers, with picnic areas and historic plaques along the waterway. The canal is once again open to vessels – but only pleasure craft and sailing boats.
*Tel: (514) 283-6054.
www.parkscanada.gc.ca/canallachine*

Rapids Park

One of the most popular stops along the Lachine bike path is directly in front of the thundering rapids that first fascinated explorer Jacques Cartier in 1535. The landscaped picnic area is the perfect spot to gain a vicarious thrill watching the rafters and kayakers who brave the raging white waters of the rapids.
500 chemin des Iroquois. Tel: (514) 364-4490. www.poledesrapides.com

Lachine Rapids Jet Boat Tours

For the past 25 years, between May and October, this company has given visitors the thrill of tackling the Lachine Rapids in a similar manner to those 18th-century explorers. You will get very, very wet – but will definitely be safer than in the old birchbark canoes. The guides aboard the *Sauté-Mouton* relate the history of the Montréal and its river until you reach the rapids – at that point the only sounds you hear will be the thunder of the whitewater and the screams of your wet companions.
Old Port of Montréal. Tel: (514) 284-9607. www.jetboatingmontreal.com

All aboard the *Sauté-Mouton*

Québec City

Clickety clack. The horse-drawn calèches seem to tap dance along the cobblestone streets. A violinist on the street corner serenades all who pass by. An artist splashes blotches of colour on her canvas as she sits on the boardwalk overlooking the scenic St Lawrence River. Where else could you be but Québec City?

This city is a monument to the history of the New World, and it radiates a special beauty and old-world charm that makes Québec unlike any other city in North America. It is this 'je ne sais quoi' that annually propels Québec into every top-ten list of favourite cities among international travellers.
Québec City Tourism. 835 avenue Wilfred-Laurier. Tel: (418) 641-6290.

Email: info@quebecregion.com.
www.quebecregion.com

Espace400e

Not content to rest on its laurels, Québec is in the process of becoming even more spectacular, with a major beautification project to celebrate the 400th anniversary of the founding of the first French settlement in Canada.

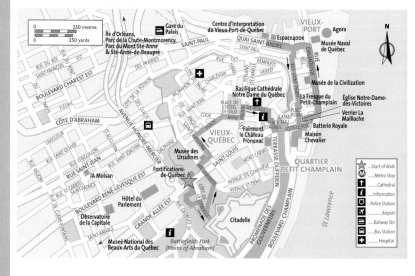

Quebéc City will be issuing an invitation to the world to join in a year-long celebration in the year 2008. This will be a party celebrating history and culture, artists and poets, chefs and their culinary creations.

1135 Grande Allée Ouest, bureau 100, Québec G1S 1E7 Canada. Tel: (418) 648-2008. www.quebecregion.com

Vieux-Québec

Vieux-Québec is the first North American urban centre – and the only walled city north of Mexico – to be added to the prestigious list of UNESCO World Heritage Sites. The walls contain four centuries of Old World history and culture along the 16th-century cobblestone streets and stone houses, This, however, is more of a 'living museum' where guests can dine in a fine restaurant or play darts in a pub that was built centuries ago. (*See Walk, p100.*)

Of particular note are the fortifications of Québec (National Historic Site), the Citadelle, Artillery Park (NHS), the Musée des Ursulines, Notre-Dame de Québec Basilica-Cathedral and the Morrin Centre/Literary and Historical Society of Québec.

Hôtel du Parlement

Though it may look as if you are still back in the time of the first explorers, these impressive buildings house the elected politicians of the National Assembly of Québec. The 125-member provincial government introduces legislation and debate policy in the exceptionally ornate National Assembly Chamber that is filled with works of art and ornamental features from past eras of Québec history. The four wings of the building were constructed in a Second Empire style between 1877 and 1886 by architect Eugène-Étienne Taché. The façade features bronze statues of 22 men and women who helped shape the future of Québec.

Above the main entrance to the parliament hangs the Québec coat of arms with the inscription 'Je me souviens' (I remember) as a guiding principle for all residents of the province (incidentally, the motto is

Hôtel du Parlement

Musée national des beaux-arts du Québec

also on every Québec licence plate). There are daily guided tours.
1045 rue des Parlementaires.
Tel: (418) 643-7239. www.assnat.qu.ca

Observatoire de la Capitale

The autumn season, with the flaming, changing colours of the Laurentide forests of maple trees, is the best time to view the capital from this 221-m (725-ft) observation balcony. However, the scenic view is magnificent any time of year; the city is laid out literally beneath your feet – Vieux-Québec, the St Lawrence, and the forests and mountains of the Laurentians just across the river. This is an excellent place for getting your bearings as you check each area against your tourist map.
Edifice Marie-Guyart 1037.

Tel: (418) 664-9841.
www.observatoirecapitale.org

Musée national des beaux-arts du Québec

While still in the Parliament Hill area, art lovers will want to visit this gallery featuring the greatest artists of Québec including Jean-Paul Ripolle and Jean-Paul Lemieux. The galleries also feature works by artists from across the country, samples of international artists and a showcase of Inuit art, both painting and sculpture. As an added bonus, the building also incorporates the city's former prison.

Parc des Champs-de-Bataille. Tel: (418) 643-2150. www.mnba.qc.ca. Open: June–Sept daily 10am–6pm. Closed: Mon in winter. Admission charge.

Quartier Petit Champlain

This is the Lower Town area of **Vieux-Québec** and it is easily reached by the funicular or staircase at the foot of the Château Frontenac. If you walk down the staircase (turn right on cote de la Montagne), do so carefully! – this is called Casse-cou ('Breakneck staircase') – and is lined with restaurants, pubs and art galleries (*see Walk, p100*).

Continued on p102.

Québec City

Vieux-Port of Québec

Walk: Upper and Lower Towns of Vieux-Québec

Whether the snow is covering the café awnings in winter white or the spring flowers are blooming on the green slopes of the Citadelle, one of the most enjoyable walks for any visitor is a meander around Vieux-Québec. (OK, if you get caught in a January blizzard, just repair to the cosy quiet of any bistro serving hot, cheesy onion soup or strawberry crêpe.)

Allow a full day. See map on p96 for route.

Start your **Upper Town** perambulations at the historic centre of it all, the 400-year-old **Fortifications-de-Québec**, at 100 rue Saint-Louis, just across the avenue Honoré Mercier from the province's **Parliament Buildings**.

You can walk beside the old city walls until you connect with the Côte de la Citadelle which will lead right into the star-shaped fortifications of the 1820 **Citadelle**, high atop Cap Diamant overlooking the St Lawrence River. It was here in 1759, on the **Plains of Abraham**, that the British defeated the French for the New World. **Battlefields Park** today is a vast oasis of green urban parkland.

From this hilltop, wander down the grassy slopes to avenue d'Auteuil and walk two blocks to rue des Ursulines (on your right) where you will find the **Musée des Ursulines** which highlights the history and charity of the nuns of the Ursuline order who arrived in 1639 to teach the young girls of New France.

From here, head up Sainte Ursuline, turn right on Sainte Anne, and left on des Jardins to the **Basilique Cathédrale Notre Dame du Québec** at the corner of rue de Buade. This is the oldest basilica in North America, established in 1647, and contains precious works of art and history in a stunning display of gilded architecture.

These are but a few of the attractions found in Upper Town and, depending on your itinerary, you may easily spend a few more days exploring the area.

But if your schedule is limited, walk a few blocks toward the massive Fairmont le Château Frontenac which fronts the Terrasse Dufferin boardwalk overlooking the St Lawrence.

From here you can take the funicular down to **Lower Town** – it's a great view but it is more fun to walk down the **Casse-cou** ('Breakneck staircase') just at the side of the hillside trolley. This is a perfect location to take photos of the colourful street.

This stone staircase take you into the heart of **du Quartier Petit Champlain**, the fun and friendly cobblestone shopping avenue of Old Town, with bars and restaurants along the way.

If you want to save your consumerism for later, turn left onto the little rue Sous-le-fort and you will find yourself in **place-Royale**, the town square of the original 17th-century settlement.

Take some time to wander around the cobblestone yard and visit the little **Église Notre-Dame-des-Victoires** (1688), the oldest stone church in North America, the **Maison Chevalier**, an example of one of the early Québecois homes, and the huge **La fresque du Petit-Champlain mural** (the corner of Notre Dame and Cote de la Montagne) which illustrates the early days of the quartier. The art of glassblowing is displayed at the **Verrier La Mailloche** – the artists create works of colourful whimsy that you can purchase when they have cooled.

A very short block away on Marche Champlain is the **Batterie Royale**, which combines the art and history of Old Québec, and introduces the visitor to the **Vieux-Port** area. Follow rue Dalhousie to the interactive archaeological displays of the **Musée de la civilisation**, and then a little further up the street to the **Musée naval de Québec**, and, finally, two blocks away on Quai Saint-Andre, the complete history and future of the port is on display at the **Centre d'interpretation du Vieux-Port-de-Québec**.

After that, take a break. Stroll back to the Quartier du Petit Champlain (via rue Saint Pierre to place-Royale) and find a little café or bistro of your choice. For a true taste of Québecois culture and tasty cuisine, join the locals at **Cochon Dingue**, their favourite restaurant right on boulevard Champlain.

Walk: Upper and Lower Towns of Vieux-Québec

Musée de la civilisation

Make sure you visit **place-Royale**, known as the birthplace of French civilisation in North America, and the **Musée de la Civilisation**.

Vieux-Port

The Old Port of Québec is a natural harbour setting where the St Lawrence River meets the fresh waters of the St Charles River; just look for the modern Cruise Line Terminal then stroll left along the waterfront. This 33-ha (82-acre) area is rich in maritime history from the early days of the first French colony along its banks. Note the stately old **Customs Building**, the open-air amphitheatre of the **Agora** and the **Merchant Navy Monument**.

J A Moisan, Épicer

Where else but Québec – the culinary capital of Canada – would you put a grocery store on a 'must see' list? Founded in 1871, J A Moisan is not only the oldest grocery in North America but still one of the best. This is a combination shop/museum that details the agri-history of Québec's produce and products with antiques, souvenirs and photos of 19th-century Québec. Moisan is a packed cornucopia of mouthwatering cuisine; an old-fashioned greengrocer, delicatessen, bakery, sweet shop, coffee corner and supplier of international food products. Sample fresh baked baguettes and pick up those coloruful Art Deco cheese

Montmorency Falls

trays. A visit to J A Moisan is a veritable feast for all the senses.

699 rue Saint-Jean.
Tel: (418) 522-0685.
www.jamoisan.com

QUÉBEC CITY ENVIRONS
Parc de la Chute-Montmorency

The highlight of this park, classified in 1994 as an historic site, is the thundering sight of Montmorency Falls that greets the visitor driving along Highway 138 a few kilometres north of Québec City. This is a staggering sight; the falls drop a dizzying 82m (272ft), which is about one-and-a-half times higher than Niagara. Visitors to the park can scale the wall and stand beside the rushing water as it soars into space and crashes in a white maelstrom far

SHRINE OF SAINTE-ANNE-DE-BEAUPRÉ

The religious and the curious from around the world have made this shrine one of the busiest and most popular attractions in the entire province; every day dozens (sometime hundreds) of tour buses fill the parking lot while thousands of visitors tour the faith-healing shrine. The first chapel was built in 1658 by Etienne Lessard, one of the first settlers in the area, as a tribute to Sainte Anne. The 'miraculous cures' were first reported in 1665 by Marie de l'Incarnation (founder of the city's Ursuline convent) when she wrote that 'paralytics walk, the blind can see again…and the sick recover their health'.

The first basilica burned the ground in 1922 and was quickly rebuilt (by architects Maxime Roisin and Louis Audet) in a spectacular medieval style, completely covered with granite; the twin towering spires soared towards the heavens and could be seen by the faithful from miles away. The interior is bathed in the soft hues of sunlight streaming through the 240 stained-glass windows of this immense shrine.

Daily Masses are presented for the faithful though the times vary throughout the year (contact the church office). There are four main highlights in a visit to Sainte-Anne:

- The Way of the Cross features lifelike figures cast in bronze and depicts the procession of Christ's final walk to Calvary (evening candlelit processions are held occasionally in July).
- The Memorial Chapel, built in 1878, displays artefacts from the early chapels on this site.
- Scala Santa, erected in 1891, contains a staircase of 28 steps symbolising the one Christ walked to face Pontius Pilate.
- Saint Anne Museum commemorates the universal devotion of the Church to Saint Anne and records the history of more than 300 years of pilgrimage to this site.

10018 avenue Royale, Sainte-Anne-de-Beaupré. Tel: (418) 827-3781. www.ssadb.qc.ca. Mass celebrated numerous times on a daily basis in both English and French. Check website for schedules.

Cyclorama de Jerusalem

This truly is a spectacle unlike any you have ever seen – the largest panoramic display in the world. This gigantic work, created in Germany between 1878 and 1882, is 14m (45ft) in height with a circumference of 110m (365ft). It creates an astonishing 360-degree illusion that the audience is actually in Jerusalem and witnessing the crucifixion. Whatever your religious affiliation, this eerie voyage to biblical times will fascinate.

8 rue Regina, Sainte-Anne-de-Beaupré. Tel: (418) 827-3101. www.cyclorama.com.
Open: daily 10am–5pm. Admission charge.

below. During spring runoff, an amazing 125,000 litres (27,500 gallons) of water per second flow over the falls. Like Niagara, one of the most impressive times to visit the park is during the winter months when the mist from the falls has turned the trees and mountainside into sculptures of ice. There are picnic areas at the base of the falls and lookout points near the summit. And don't miss the gondola ride that will sweep you in front of the falls high above the churning waters.
2490 avenue Royale.
Tel: (418) 663-3330.
www.sepaq.com/chutemontmorency

Mont-Sainte-Anne

Most city-dwellers have to drive for hours to indulge their passion for downhill skiing. Québec City residents have professionally designated slopes in their own backyard. Mont-Sainte-Anne, registered on the World Cup Circuit, has more than 40 downhill runs, suitable for the novice and the expert. The park itself maintains an interconnecting 212-km (132-mile) system of groomed cross-country trails. This is also one of the most popular camping grounds in the summer – book early for any of the 166 serviced pitches. Don't miss the spectacular view of the St Lawrence when the summer gondola ascends an 800-m (2,625-ft) incline to transport hikers, mountain bikers and picnickers along the mountaintop.

2000 boulevard du Beau-Pré.
Tel: (418) 872-3121.
www.mont-sainte-anne.com

Île d'Orléans

This little island in the St Lawrence, where the saltwater tides meet and mingle with the freshwater river currents, is known as the birthplace of francophones in North America. The first 300 families from the Old World settled on this tiny island centuries ago and turned it into one of the nation's finest agricultural centres. The island itself, positioned between the Appalachian Mountains and the Canadian Shield, has always been known for its rich, fertile soil and excellent agricultural produce; fishing, of course, has always been excellent. Most of the fresh produce served in restaurants from Montréal to Tadoussac comes from the Île d'Orléans. The farms on the island are also known for raising plump juicy ducks for that excellent foie gras only available in Québec City and the Charlevoix region.

These days the island's 7,000 inhabitants have added a casual tourism industry to their island lifestyle, welcoming people who wish to tour the farmlands, hike or cycle along the trails and pathways, throw a line off any shoreline (the host at any of the island's establishments will cook it for your dinner) or just relax for a weekend of wining and dining with the freshest produce possible.

The Taschereau Bridge, just east of Chute Montmorency, connects this island 'Garden of Québec' to the mainland via Highway 138 a mere 8km (5 miles) downstream from Québec City.

Île d'Orléans Tourist Information. 490 cote du Pont, Saint-Pierre-de-Île-d'Orléans.
Tel: (418) 828-9411.
www.iledorleans.com

View over Île d'Orléans

Ski Québec

Although the Province of Ontario has its fair share of ski hills and plenty of winter resorts – specifically in the Collingwood and Barrie areas, just north of Toronto – most people in this Anglo province head for the slopes of Québec for their winter fun. As for the residents of Québec, they just remain in their province to enjoy the winter.

There are three main ski areas in Québec – **the Laurentians**, the **Eastern Townships** and the **Greater Québec area**.

Montréalers are fortunate to have the first two in their backyards – the

Laurentians are about an hour's drive to the north along Highway 15, while the Eastern Townships are about the same distance due east along Highway 10.

There are five main mountain and resort regions in the four-season playground of the Laurentians: **Mont Tremblant** (vertical 649m/2,129ft), **Gray Rocks** (189m/620ft), **Mont Blanc** (300m/984ft), **Mont Saint Sauveur** (213m/699ft) and **Ski Chantecler** (183m/600ft). The largest and most popular, Mont Tremblant (*see p110*), boasts a total of 92 downhill trails and can handle

Head to Québec for some skiing

The easy way back to the top!

Québec City residents only need drive north for 20 minutes along Highway 175 before they reach **Stoneham** (420m/1,378ft), or another 20 minutes to **Mont Sainte Anne** (625m/2,050ft). About 14,000 skiers an hour have access to the 30 trails of Stoneham, while 19,000 skiers per hour can schuss down Mont Sainte Anne's 56 runs.

Residents also have the option of driving east along Highway 138 into the **Charlevoix region** to take advantage of the 720-m (2,362-ft) vertical slopes of **Le Massif Ski Resort** – the highest ski drop in the province with the most spectacular view of the St Lawrence River far below.

Since the resorts are so close to these major cities, many residents just drive out for the day. However, if you decide to treat yourself to a weekend getaway, there are excellent resorts, chalets, hotels, motels, B&Bs and – for the younger, more budget-conscious – ski hostels in each major winter region. And since this is Québec, the visitor can expect some excellent cuisine and wine in the hotel dining room or any little roadside diner. Even the poutine (*see p116*) tastes better in the crisp cold of the Québec winter.

approximately 25,000 skiers per hour. The smallest in this region, Gray Rocks, lists 22 trails for a maximum of 5,000 skiers per hour. Gray Rocks has always been known as hosting the best 'ski school' in the country.

The second most popular winter region is the Eastern Townships with popular resorts including **Mont Sutton** (460m/1,509ft), **Mont Orford** (540m/1,772ft), **Owl's Head** (540m/1,772ft) and **Bromont** (405m/1,329ft). The largest, Mont Sutton, features 53 trails and carries 12,000 skiers an hour, while the smallest, Bromont, can distribute 5,000 skiers an hour to its 45 mountain trails.

For complete winter information and packages, contact:
Tourisme Québec.
www.bonjourquebec.com

Laurentians

This is the playground for Montréalers and for many citizens of the United States who live on the south banks of the St Lawrence Seaway. The Laurentians is a 22,000-sq km (849-sq mile) four-season resort area of sleepy little French villages, of hillside ski chalets and palatial country estates, country inns and shoreline cottages, lakes for swimming or ice fishing, forest trails for hiking or cross-country skiing and parks for overnight camping or afternoon picnics. For most visitors, however, the Laurentians conjures up images of a white winter with snow-covered ski hills.

'Le P'tit Train du Nord' Linear Park

This 'linear' park stretches 200km (124 miles) from St Jerome in the south to Mont-Laurier in the northwest region of the Laurentians. The path, now designed for cyclists, skaters and cross-country skiers, follows the tracks of the famous 'little train of the north' that opened up the inaccessible wilderness between Montréal and the interior of the Laurentians.

14 142 de la Chapelle, Mirabel.

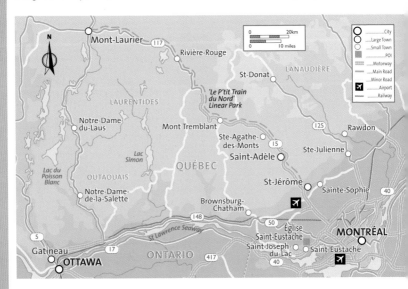

Tel: (450) 224-7007.
www.laurentides.com. Check for
changing train schedules and prices.

Église Saint-Eustache

Located in Saint-Eustache, the first
town of the Laurentians, this historic
church was first built in the year 1783
but was virtually demolished a few
years later in a battle between the
French and British armies. The semi-
cylindrical design has created such
unique acoustics that the Montréal
Symphony Orchestra has made this its
recording studio for the past 20 years.
123 rue Saint-Louis.
Tel: (450) 473-3200 (x234).
Email: eglise@st-eustache.hn.org

Gourmet Trail/Laurentians

The three participating components of
the Laurentians' gastronomic route
include farms, restaurants and fine food
shops. The farm tours include the
organic produce of Les Jardins de
l'Achillee Millefeuille, the free-range
organic chicken and beef of Ferme
Picardier, and the Barbary duck and
guinea fowl of Ferme Morgan.
Tel: (819) 688-7335.
www.montsetdelices.com

Les Fromagiers de la Table Ronde

Cheese lovers from all over the world
come to Québec to sample and
purchase its speciality cheeses.
317 route 158, Sainte-Sophie.
Tel: (450) 530-2436.
www.fromagiersdelatableronde.qc.ca.

Open: June–Sept daily from 10am.
Free admission.

À la Chocolaterie Marie-Claude

The employees of this traditional
chocolate shop and café take pride in
creating chocolate delicacies by hand,
using old country-style techniques.
1090 rue Valiquette, Saint-Adele.
Tel: (450) 229-3991.
www.laurentides.com.
Open: Dec–Oct Thur–Sun daily
10am–5pm. Free admission.

Vignoble La Roche des Brises

Any visitor might think they have been
transported to a Californian vineyard
when sitting on the hillside of Vignoble
La Roche des Brises. The winery gives
tours of the vineyards and orchards as
well as the production facilities.
200 chemin Principal, Saint-Joseph-du-
Lac. Tel: (450) 472-2722.
www.rochedesbrises.com. Open:
May–Sept daily. Free admission. Guided
tours arranged by request.

Église Saint-Eustache

Mont Tremblant Ski Resort

For enthusiasts of winter, particularly downhill skiing, Mont Tremblant is the heart and soul of the Laurentians and justifiably boasts the best skiing in Canada east of Alberta's Rocky Mountains. The resort itself is consistently voted number one in Québec – not only for its many winter amenities but also as a summer destination for golfers and tennis players.

The mountain is a mere one-and-a-half-hour drive from Montréal (sharing a border with the national park), so winter weekends are packed with skiers, snowboarders and cross-country enthusiasts.

The Algonquin tribe named Mont Tremblant Monitonga Soutera (Mountain of the Spirit), and it was discovered in the 1920s by the Red Bird Ski Club in Montréal. This group, led by Jackrabbit Johansen, would take the 'P'tit Train du Nord' and climb the mountain wearing cross-country skis!

The first resort was built in 1939 by an eccentric American millionaire and has been slowly expanded over the years. However, the real boom came in 1991 when Canadian company IntraWest, the largest investor in alpine resorts, decided to turn Tremblant into one of the world's great ski resorts.

Today Tremblant is a statistical dream for any skier. The elevation of the mountain is 875m (2,871ft), the vertical drop is 645m (2,116ft) and there is a massive 254ha (628 acres) of skiable slope to tackle.

Any level of skier will always find challenges in Tremblant's 94 trails (the longest at 6km/3³/4 miles). There are 17 trails for beginners, 33 for intermediate and 50 for the expert (read: fearless) crowd.

The average annual snowfall is a whopping 382cm (150in) which guarantees a well-packed natural base from November to April, while the 870 snowmaking guns create fresh fluffy snow every night for the early-morning crowds.

And since this is Québec, food and drink are a natural part of any activity – the skier can stop in for strawberry crêpes at the summit (Crepe Bretonne), steak et frites at la Fourchette du Diable on the north side, or perhaps some poutine at le Chateau du Voyages or Johannsen on the south slopes.

Tremblant also offers acres of Snow Parks, several areas where snowboarders can practise their leaps and mid-air twists off ramps and rails, as well as an Olympic-calibre super-pipe for those eyeing the next Winter Olympic Games.

But one of the most enjoyable runs of the day is the official ski tour of the area (9.30am and 1.30pm), presented by one of the local ski instructors/guides who will give you the history and folklore of the area during a 60-minute exploration of the mountain.

Accommodation? No problem. There are thousands of rooms available in the area, ranging from luxury resort rooms and mountainside chalets to little B&Bs and youth hostels.

1000 chemin des Voyaguers.
Tel: (888) 289-8888. www.tremblant.ca

Mont Tremblant Ski Resort

Charlevoix region

'Ah, Charlevoix.' This region is magical for Québecers; just mention the word and watch their eyes glaze over as they conjure up fond memories of cosy country inns, dozens of little art galleries, stunning, colourful scenery and long leisurely seven-course dinners. This gorgeous area has become a mecca for painters, writers and musicians who have been inspired by the natural beauty for centuries. Charlevoix stretches 215km (134 miles) northeast along the St Lawrence from Québec City to Tadoussac.

Most of the 30,000 inhabitants are artists and artisans with workshops, boutiques, studios and galleries filling every second shopfront in little francophone villages such as Baie-Saint-Paul, La Malbaie and Notre-Dame-des-Monts.
www.tourisme-charlevoix.com

The Gourmet Route/La Table Agro-Touristique

This winding tour of culinary discovery includes local specialities such as indigenous cheeses available only in the region (look for Ciel de Charlevoix, a blue-veined cheese), smoked fish and the locally produced 'blue potato'.

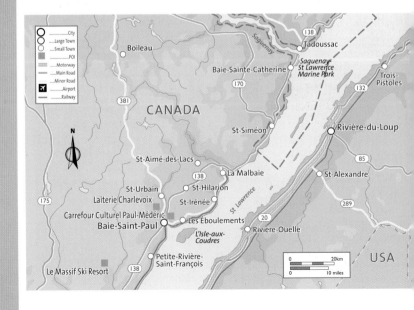

Guests visit speciality farms that raise emu, churn cheese and fatten ducks for the exquisite fois gras of Charlevoix.
www.gourmetroute.com

Le Massif Ski Resort

This region is also popular as a winter retreat. Many winter enthusiasts from Québec, as well as those south of the border in the United States, will visit Charlevoix for a week of winter activities including cross-country skiing (the area boasts miles of beautifully groomed country trails), snowmobiling, dog sledding, ice skating and even romantic rides in an old wooden horse-drawn sleigh.

Most of these winter activities are centred around Le Massif Ski Resort – at 7,699m (2,526ft) the highest vertical drop east of the Canadian Rockies. The view from the top is stunning as the skier overlooks the crisp cold blue of the St Lawrence River. There are 42 trails ranging from gently winding beginner slopes to the advanced adrenaline runs of rough terrain and bumpy moguls.
1350 rue Principale. Petite-Rivière-Saint-François. Tel: (418) 632-5876. Email: hmoreau@lemassif.com.
www.lemassif.com. Open: Dec–Mar daily 9am–4pm. Basic day ticket, but the facility offers numerous rates and packages.

Baie-Saint-Paul

This is the first village that greets the visitor from Québec City – right off Highway 138. The colourful town is packed with art galleries, crafts boutiques and cosy restaurants with prices unlike any tourist town you have ever seen. (A very filling five-course meal of 'steak et frites' including soup, salad, coffee and dessert is exceedingly inexpensive at Le Rustique Pub.) Also, collectors of local art will find themselves spending hours in the little galleries, often discussing the works with the artists themselves; some of the galleries are set up in the front parlours of the artists' homes.

Carrefour Culturel Paul-Médéric

Dedicate some time to this gallery in the village that highlights the best of Charlevoix's heritage and performing and visual arts.
4 rue Amboise-Fafard.
Tel: (418) 435-2540. Email: carrefourculturel@baiesaintpaul.com.
www.baiesaintpaul.com

Laiterie Charlevoix

It is not often one finds a museum dedicated to cheese, but it is a 'must see', and taste, for any visitor. The Cheese Economuseum is just off Highway 138, right before Baie-Saint-Paul. It started as a little dairy in 1948 and has expanded to demonstrate the many stages of the cheese-making process.
1167 boulevard Mgr-De Laval.
Tel: (418) 435-2184.
www.fromagescharlevoix.com. Open: daily 10am–5pm.
Free admission.

L'Isle-aux-Coudres

A tiny island in the St Lawrence, only a few minutes' ferry ride from either Baie-Saint-Paul or Saint-Joseph-de-la-Rive, L'Isle-aux-Coudres is a perfect microcosm of the pastoral beauty of Charlevoix. This is the ideal quiet retreat for walking, hiking, bird-watching, fishing, painting and just relaxing. The best way to see the island is by bicycle – it's a pleasant, meandering 26-km (16-mile) ride around the entire shoreline – and there are some lovely art galleries and restaurants along the circumference. Many people spend the weekend in rustic country inns or campsites while indulging in some of Québec's finest restaurants.

La Malbaie

'Bad Bay' is the largest town of the Charlevoix and is located exactly in the middle of the region, hugging the shoreline of the St Lawrence, the commercial lifeline for the town. The area was named in 1608 by explorer Samuel de Champlain whose ship was stuck in the bay when the water disappeared during low tide. ('Ah, la malle baye', cried the dismayed captain.) Today things have changed – although the daily tide still leaves the boats stranded – and the area is populated by tourists on the golf course, and in the casino and art galleries.

The Musée de Charlevoix

Located in La Malbaie, this is the most visited museum/gallery in the entire region. Founded in 1975, the museum has a mandate to 'preserve and showcase' the works of artists and craftspeople throughout the Charlevoix area. Those interested in original souvenirs will also want to spend time in the Boutique which carries popular folk art and signed works by artisans from Charlevoix and other areas of the province.
10 chemin du Havre. Tel: (418) 665-4411. Open: July and Aug daily 9am–5pm. Closed: Mon Sept–June. Admission charge.

Fairmont Le Manoir Richelieu Hotel

This is a spectacular example of one of North America's wilderness 'grand dame' hotels. Founded in 1899 by the Canadian Pacific Railway, the massive manor received a $140-million

La Malbaie

renovation in 1999 that restored the hotel to its former 1920s glory. It was used as a country escape by high-society mavens from New York, Boston, Montréal and Toronto who arrived by steamship and rail. The modern additions include a professional 18-hole golf course – open to the public. This 405-room hotel, with its three restaurants, two bars and even a Cigar Room, boasts a stunning view of the St Lawrence River.
181 rue Richelieu. Tel: (418) 665-3703. www.fairmont.com

Whale-watching

Casino de Charlevoix
Located just across the road from Le Manoir Richelieu is this European-style casino, which contains 20 gaming tables (blackjack, roulette, etc.) and almost 800 slot machines. The casino is open all year round and guests must be over 18.
183 rue Richelieu.
Tel: (418) 665-5300.

Saguenay-St Lawrence Marine Park/Tadoussac
This stunning marine park is one of the most unusual in the world. The first park in Québec created to protect its exclusive marine environment, ranging from sea lions to beluga whales, it covers part of the St Lawrence Seaway and the mysterious Saguenay Fjord. There are interpretive centres scattered throughout the park; visitors can join a regularly scheduled tour or simply hike by themselves along the spectacular

cliffs overlooking the frolicking seals. There are also areas where you can go underground and observe the sea creatures in their natural habitat.
Parcs Canada. 182 rue de l'Église, Tadoussac. Tel: (418) 235-4703. www.parcmarin.qc.ca.
Open: June–Sept daily 10am–5pm. Admission charge.

Whale watching/fjord cruises
Various cruise lines in the Tadoussac/ Baie-Sainte-Catherine area provide watery excursions into the spectacular Saguenay Fjord (with its stunning 244-m/800-ft waterfall), as well as allowing you to skim the waters in a tiny 12-seat Zodiac. Tours sail between May and October.
Croisieres 2001 Inc.
www.croisieres2001.com
Les pionniers de la baleine.
www.baleines.ca. May–Oct only.
Numerous cruises, packages and schedules.

Poutine and tortière

Poutine

Poutine (pronounced 'Poo-Teen') is a French-Canadian dish that combines French fried potatoes, thick chicken gravy and chewy curds of cheese in one delightful mess. It was created in 1957 by restaurateur Fernand Lachance, in Warwick, Québec, a town with the reputation of producing the best cheese curds in the country.

There is an accepted method of preparing the best poutine. The potatoes must be very fresh, hand-cut and fried in pure lard. The gravy (actually BBQ chicken gravy) is quite dark, very hot and as thick as molasses – the chef must be able to stand a spoon straight up in the gravy.

The final ingredient – the cheese – is the most important part of good poutine: you must use very fresh, white, cheddar cheese curds. The curds have a taste all their own, very different to a block of cheddar cheese. The cheese curds must squeak (!) as you bite into them.

To assemble the dish you start with the fries, then add the curds and finally pour over the gravy.

Poutine is readily available across Canada, but it only really tastes good in French Québec. In Montréal, check out the fast-food chain called LaFleur ('the flower') for good poutine. It's much easier to find in Québec City – look for a sign in front of any restaurant that features a bucket of fries. Outside the cities, stop at an old-fashioned 'chip wagon' along the side of the road or in the middle of every little town. These are the best 'frites' you will ever taste.

Tortière

This savoury meat pie is a classic Québecois dish traditionally served at family gatherings or on the eve of special occasions, especially Christmas. The following is from an old family cookbook collected from Montréal by Cherie Veau Barbière.

- 225g ($^1/_2$lb) lean ground beef
- 225g ($^1/_2$lb) ground pork
- 1 onion, chopped
- 1 clove garlic
- $^1/_2$ tsp salt
- $^1/_2$ tsp savory or thyme
- $^1/_2$ tsp celery salt
- $^1/_2$ tsp ground cloves
- $^1/_2$ cup water
- $^1/_2$ cup breadcrumbs
- uncooked pie shell

In a saucepan mix together the lean ground beef and the ground pork, add all the other ingredients (except the breadcrumbs) and bring to the boil.

Turn down, and simmer for 20 minutes.

Add $1/2$ cup breadcrumbs, spoon by spoon, until the fat is absorbed.

Cool the mixture.

Pour into an uncooked pie shell.

Add the top crust. Bake for 25 minutes in a preheated 450°F (gas mark 8/230°C) oven.

Cool before serving.

Poutine

The Gaspé Peninsula

It is impossible to get lost if you take an eastern drive (starting on the northern shoreline) around the circumference of the Gaspé (also known as the Gaspésie) Peninsula – there will be water on your left-hand side until you bump into the Atlantic province of New Brunswick about 800km (497 miles) later.

This rugged shoreline touches water on three sides: the St Lawrence Seaway, the Gulf and the Baie des Chaleurs. The Gaspé, about the size of Belgium, records a mere 140,000 inhabitants. This is a largely unpopulated area for wilderness discovery, a tourism destination for the adventurous. There are little coastal fishing villages and sea

shanties, lakeside picnic areas and quiet forest reserves, cliffs and meadows to explore. You can listen to fishermen's tales at night around a fireplace in a cosy little B&B, or camp at Land's End, waking in the morning to the sight of whales frolicking in the Gulf of St Lawrence. There are five regions within the Gaspé: The Coast, The Haute-

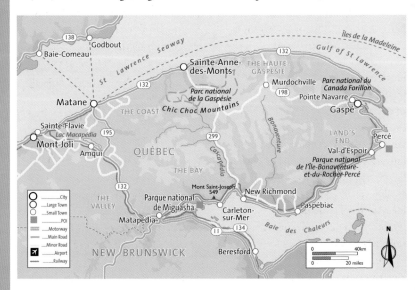

Gaspésie, Land's End, The Bay and The Valley.

Gaspésie Tourism. 357 route de la Mer, Sainte-Flavie. Tel: (418) 775-2223. www.tourisme-gaspesie.com

THE COAST
Sainte-Flavie

This small village (population almost 1,000) serves as the gateway to the Gaspé Peninsula. There is a bird sanctuary, a cultural centre here and even a palaeontology museum, but you should also visit the auberge, bistro Marée bleue, for your first taste of fish or seafood à la Gaspésie.
www.municipalite-sainteflavie.qc.ca

Matane

This is the largest community (population 15,000) along the Coast region and a true fishing one – just wander along the Matane-sur-Mer harbour with its fleet of fishing tugs, sailing boats and ferry service. The ferry service traverses the Seaway to the north coast of the province as well as to the Îles-de-la-Madeleine in the middle of the Seaway. Also at the harbour you can tour the plant that specialises in the famous 'Matane shrimp' and pick up information on the area at the old lighthouse, now a tourist centre.

While in Matane, make sure you visit the Mathieu-d'Amours Dam (Observation Centre for the salmon run), where you can watch the Atlantic salmon 'run' through underground Plexiglas viewing pods. The Matane River also offers 81 pools for salmon fishing.

Les Jardins de Doris are relaxing rock gardens (the Gaspésie is part of the Appalachian mountain range) with numerous fruit trees, perennials and shrubs. There is also a small petting zoo for children here.

THE HAUTE-GASPÉSIE
Sainte-Anne-des-Monts
Parc national de la Gaspésie

This provincial park on the summit of the Chic Choc Mountains (a continuation of the Appalachians) towers above the verdant boreal forests and deep blue rivers and provides a stunning panorama of the protected miles of parkland far below. With 140km (87 miles) of trails, this is the ideal area for hiking and cross-country skiing. In addition, you are practically guaranteed to see caribou and herds of moose. Services include fishing, canoeing and well-equipped picnic areas. The 800-sq km (309-sq mile) park claims 25 of the highest summits in the province.

1981 route du parc, Sainte-Anne-des-Monts. www.sepaq.com

Exploramer, la mer à découvrir

This fascinating interactive complex features the marine activity of the St Lawrence River. It is a 'garden under the sea' where visitors can view living marine and plant life in its natural habitat. There are also a dozen aquariums and tanks that contain the natural mysteries of the river – fish and flowing plant life – unseen to those on the shore. Don't miss the thrill of the covered Zodiac ride (maximum 18 passengers) which zooms through the waters to the playground of the beluga whales.

1 rue du Quai, Sainte-Anne-des-Monts. Tel: (418) 763-2500. www.exploramer.org

Percé Rock

LAND'S END

Parc national du Canada Forillon

Although the official designation of Land's End makes this region sound slightly ominous, Forillon Park is an area filled with astonishing flora and fauna, and rich human and cultural history. You can escape into the middle of a leafy green nowhere and enjoy the total seclusion of nature or, alternatively, enjoy the summer activities of snorkelling, scuba diving, horse riding, biking and tennis. Both seals and whales frolic along the shoreline of Forillon but the guides at the Interpretation Centre warn you to beware of the porcupines. Make sure you hike out to the old lighthouse at the tip of Cap-Bon-Aux, the furthest tip of the Gaspé jutting out into the Gulf of St Lawrence. And campers take note: there are 367 partially serviced pitches in the park and several wilderness camping areas.

122 boulevard de Gaspé, Gaspé. Tel: (418) 368-5505. www.pc.gc.ca/forillon

Gaspé

The town of Gaspé itself, at the mid-point in your drive, is a perfect spot to stop for a few days to explore the past while visiting a community with a summer season of weekly festivals, art shows, fishing derbies and French hospitality. In the original native Micmac, the word Gespeg translates as 'end of the land'; however, for explorer Jacques Cartier, it was the Cradle of Canada. (The town has both a

monument and museum to the 'discoverer of the New World'.) The municipality is made up of 17 coastal villages that have preserved their old-world francophone ethnic and cultural traditions over the years.
www.tourismegaspe.org

Site d'interpretation de la culture Micmac de Gespeg

This re-created village was designed to allow guests an insight into the daily life of the Micmac tribe circa 1675. The Micmac had the reputation of being a peaceful and resourceful people who lived in close harmony with nature, creating clothing and tools from available natural resources. The 'End of the Land' interpretive centre and Micmac guides explain the history of the people, their beliefs and legends in both French and English.
783 boulevard Pointe-Navarre, Gaspé.
Tel: (418) 368-7449.
www.micmacgespeg@globetrotter.net

Percé

This little village of the Gaspé seems to attract artists and birders who flock here every season. The town itself is a haven for adventure activities including diving and kayaking as well as naturalist activities such as whale watching. There are plenty of inns and motels in the area, but many people camp in the adjacent Parc national de l'Île-Bonaventure-et-du-Rocher-Percé.
www.perce.info

Parc national de l'Île-Bonaventure-et-du-Rocher-Percé

The park wardens, who are trained naturalists, will guide you through the flora and fauna of Bonaventure – a paradise for nature lovers. The colony of 120,000 northern gannets is the most important colony in North America and the most accessible in the world.
www.perce.info

Centre d'interprétation et de formation agroécologique

The CIFA in Val-d'Espoir commemorates the old Gaspésie traditions of sustainable agriculture: fish and seafood were plentiful but farmers had to develop special techniques to grow crops on this rocky region of the province. Surprisingly, given the rugged landscape, there are also numerous gardens of ornamental and colourful flowers and plants that seem to grow right out of the rocks. Note the medicinal plants that residents of Gaspé have used for centuries for natural home remedies.
397 route des Peres, Val-d'Espoir.
Tel: (418) 782-2777.
www.biojardins.com

THE BAY
Paspébiac

The Bay area is an official member of The Most Beautiful Bays in the World Club. This organisation started in Germany in 1997 with a mandate to promote and protect natural global heritage sites. Paspébiac is one of the best places to enjoy the Bay area in all its stunning scenic splendour. The beach area has a boardwalk near the crashing waves, while the hiking trails along the cliffs provide an excellent view of the village's natural curved harbour.

www.paspebiac.com

Site Historique du Banc-de-Peche-de-Paspébiac

The site, recognised as an historic site by Heritage Canada, comprises 11 buildings that for centuries exported dry-salted cod worldwide before refrigeration and rapid transportation. This commercial fishing venture helped promote the development of fisheries in both Québec and the Atlantic Provinces. The bilingual guides demonstrate the history of the area through story-telling and fishermen's tales of the sea. The centre still produces samples of salted cod for its visitors.

Third Street, Paspébiac. Tel: (418) 752-6408. Email: shbp@globetrotter.net

Gaspésian British Heritage Village

Located in New Richmond, this historic village celebrates the arrival of the new immigrants from the British Isles more than two centuries ago. Some of the historic buildings include the Willett general store, the original post office, hardware store, school and blacksmith shop, which you can visit on a horse-drawn carriage ride through the village. There is even a genealogy centre if you

lost some ancestors several hundred years ago. The French and British lived together in peace in the Gaspé region – the Anglo-Franco wars carried on without them.

351 boulevard Perron Ouest, New Richmond. Tel: (418) 392-4487. www.villenewrichmond.com

Oratoire Notre-Dame-du-Mont-Saint-Joseph

Sitting completely alone, overlooking the rugged shoreline of the Bay and community of Carleton-sur-Mer, the oratory, built in 1935, dominates the top of Mont-Saint-Joseph (555m/ 1,820ft). Inside is filled with incredible mosaics, dazzling stained-glass windows and solid marble artwork. Guided tours are available.

837 rue de la Montagne, Carleton. Tel: (418) 364-2256. www.carletonsuremer.com

Parc national de Miguasha

Scholars and archaeologists from all over the world come here to study the animal, fish and plant life that has been frozen in time in the cliffs. These fossils, dating back some 378 million years, have been remarkably preserved – the fossils of the Miguasha fish have helped scholars chart the transition of vertebrates from aquatic to terrestrial life. Guided tours take the visitor through a teaching laboratory as well as along the fossilised cliffs (note: not accessible to people with reduced mobility). The museum has also produced an educational, animated film (*Journey Deep into the Origins*) that runs throughout the day in the amphitheatre. This exceptional natural park is a UNESCO World Heritage Site. *231 route Miguasha Ouest, Nouvelle.* *Tel: (418) 794-2475.* *www.sepaq.com*

THE VALLEY
Matapédia

Tucked away in the corner of the Baie des Chaleurs, just a stone's throw from the Province of New Brunswick, this tiny town of just 737 inhabitants is known primarily as the Québec gateway to the international Appalachian Trail. And yes, every year thousands of people spend their holiday hiking hundreds of kilometres along this incredible mountainous pathway. Non-hikers, however, can sample some of the best salmon fishing in the world, or enjoy swimming and boating along the Matapédia and Restigouche rivers. Winter enthusiasts will find all they need at Le Petit Chamonix ski resort. *www.gaspesie.net/matapedia*

St Lawrence rocks, Gaspé Peninsula

Îles de la Madeleine

This archipelago is located more than 200km (124 miles) from the east coast of Gaspé and 125km (78 miles) north of Prince Edward Island. In fact the islanders are far enough away from the mainland that they live in a different time zone – one hour ahead of the rest of the province. The Îles de la Madeleine (not part of the Gaspé Peninsula) boast their own tourism organisation even though few tourists make it to their shores. Which is a shame because this is truly one of the most fascinating regions in the province.

The islands and their people

There are a dozen islands in this group and six are connected to one another by long, thin sand dunes. The main islands are Île de la Grande Entrée, Grosse Isle, Île aux Loups, Île du Havre aux Maisons, Île du Cap aux Meules and Île Havre Aubert. (The largest island, Havre Aubert, is only about 12km/7^1/$_2$ miles long.) This remains a francophone culture, a mixture of Québec and Acadian influences; listen to the melodic notes of the Acadian accent, similar to the Cajun speech of Louisiana. The islanders, all 13,172 of them, have a history of proud isolation but that certainly doesn't mean they aren't friendly. Just the opposite, in fact; any new face is obviously a stranger and the locals are more than pleased to tell you about their island home in the middle of the Gulf of St Lawrence.

The mainstay of the islands' economy is, naturally, commercial fishing, which brings in fresh daily supplies of lobster, scallops, snow crabs, cod, shark and all types of shellfish; fish and seafood don't get any fresher than this.

History

The first inhabitants of the islands in 1755 were the Acadians who reached these shores following their exile from the mainland. They were joined some years later by French settlers from St Pierre and Miquelon and over the years (so legend has it) also by sailors who were shipwrecked on these rocky shores and decided to make the islands their home.

Visiting the islands

It is easy to explore all the islands – for those which you can't walk to across the sandbars, there are regular ferry boats between the main islands and villages. Activities include everything from hiking, biking, fishing, bird-watching, seal sightings and just soaking up the culture and cuisine of a slower-paced society from another era.

The climate is surprisingly temperate due to the huge water masses that encompass the archipelago and create milder conditions for each season. And even though you are in the middle of the ocean, you can still swim in the (admittedly) refreshing 20°C (68°F) waters of the lagoons and bays of Madeleine.

There is ferry service to the Îles de la Madeleine from 21 different locations in Québec (check the website for various departure points and times) as well as from Prince Edward Island. Visitors can also fly if they don't want to face the unpredictable waters of the St Lawrence.

Island accommodation runs the complete gamut from five-star hotels and B&Bs to rental homes and youth hostels.

Îles de la Madeleine. 128 chemin Principal, Cap-aux-Meules, Québec. Tel: (418) 986-2245 or (877) 624-4437.
www.tourismeilesdelamadeleine.com

Îles de la Madeleine coastline

Getting away from it all

Since Canada is the second-largest country in the world by landmass and 85 per cent of the (approximately 30 million) population live within 240km (150 miles) of the shared border between Canada and the United States, there is a vast and unpopulated wilderness of forests and prairies between the coasts of the Atlantic and Pacific.

Most visitors to Québec stay within close driving range of the St Lawrence Seaway in their exploration of the province or en route to Canada's four Atlantic provinces. Only those interested in 'communing with the wild' – camping on a lake shore with only the loons for company or canoeing along uninhabited stretches of lakes and rivers – tackle the wilderness interior of Québec.

Ontario, on the other hand, has towns and cities along the 2,000km (1,243 miles) of highways and roads north and west to the Manitoba border.

The resort town of Bracebridge

Flowerpot Island near Tobermory

Tobermory

This little town on the tip of land where the waters of Georgian Bay and Lake Huron meet is home to Fathom Five Park, known as the freshwater diving capital of the world, complete with shipwrecks, huge sea bass and flowerpot islands. It is also where non-divers pick up the car ferry to Manitoulin Island (*tel: (519) 596-2452; www.tobermory.org*).

Manitoulin Island

The Ontario Northland ferry, the Chi Cheemaun (Big Canoe), transports passengers and vehicles to Manitoulin Island, the world's largest island (2,700sq km/1,042sq miles) in a freshwater lake, from the mainland harbour to the little town of South Baymouth. Many visitors spend some

days exploring the native roots of the island and visiting the little villages of Spring Bay, Kagawong, Manitowaning, Wikwemikong or Two O'Clock. Indians believed this sacred island was the home of The Great Spirit, Gitchi-Manitou; every year Native tribes come from all over North America to take part in a combined Pow Wow of respect for the 'Old Ways' and legends. The ferry to the northern mainland leaves from Little Current.

Manitoulin Island. www.manitoulin.ca; www.manitoulin-island.com
Chi Cheemaun Car Ferry. Tel: (800) 265-3163; www.ontarioferries.com

Kilarney Provincial Park

Just as you leave the ferry on the north side of Manitoulin Island, you will see signs for Kilarney Provincial Park, often

St Joseph Island

referred to as the 'crown jewel' of Ontario's park system. The park consists of 342sq km (132sq miles) of wilderness anchored to the southern tip of the Canadian Shield, perfect for canoeing, camping and hiking, and an artistic inspiration to Canada's Group of Seven (*see p35*).
www.ontarioparks.com/english/kill.html

Sudbury

Home of Canada's mining industry, Sudbury can be seen for miles away due to its 380-m (1,247-ft) high Copper Cliff smokestack, the tallest in the world, and is represented by a 9-m (29-ft) high 1951 Canadian commemorative coin just as you enter the town. The mines offer underground museum tours of the process.
Sudbury Tourism. Tel: (705) 671-2487; www.city.greatersudbury.on.ca

St Joseph Island

This little island (30km by 24km/ 19 miles by 15 miles) is the perfect place to rest for a day or so, especially if you want to swim, fish, sail or even explore old historic sites – the ruins of the most westerly military fort in Upper Canada, built in 1796, are preserved today in the Fort St Joseph National Historic Site. The island is connected to the mainland by one bridge just off Trans Canada Highway 17.
St Joseph Island Chamber of Commerce. www.stjosephisland.net

Sault Ste Marie

Known by all Canadians as 'The Soo', this is the country's second-largest producer of steel (after Hamilton, Ontario). Its twin city on the American side of the border, also called Sault Ste Marie, links Lake Huron with Lake

Superior, making this an important and historical port city: the lock systems on both sides of the border are the busiest in the world. Take time to visit the MS *Norgama* – the last passenger ship on the Great Lakes – that has now been turned into a marine history museum. This is also where passengers board the Algoma Central Railway for a one-day trip north into the incredible scenic Agawa Canyon – about two hours away in Lake Superior Provincial Park. This is one of the world's great train trips (the only way to get into this area is by train). The colours are spectacular in the autumn but the winter wilderness white is equally breathtaking (*www.agawacanyon.com*). *Sault Ste Marie Tourism.*

Tel: (705) 949-7152; www.city.sault-ste-marie.on.ca

Lake Superior Provincial Park

Highway 17 now meanders through this huge, 1,554sq km (600sq miles) provincial park that provides plenty of roadside campsites for an afternoon picnic or overnight stay. *www.ontarioparks.com/English/lakes.html*

Wawa

A massive 9-m (29$^1/_2$-ft) high Goose will greet you upon entering the town of Wawa. The steel structure salutes not only the thousands upon thousands of migrating geese that fly over this little town of 5,000 every autumn but also the name itself – Wawa means 'wild

Getting away from it all

Agawa Canyon

goose' in native Ojibaway. Iron ore and tourism are Wawa's basic economic mainstays.
Wawa Tourism. www.wawa.cc

Pukaskwa National Park

Yet another huge park along the highway. Take time to visit the Gibson Lake where Schist Falls drops 260m (835ft) into the gorge as it runs off into Lake Superior.
www.pc.gc.ca/pn-np/on/pukaskwa/ index_E.asp

Rossport

This tiny little community offers old-style lodging in the Rossport Inn, one of the little railway inns that offered rest and relaxation on those long train trips in the early years of the 20th century. This is also one of the most scenic viewpoints you will have

Kakabeka Falls

of the little islands in the massive Lake Superior.
Rossport Inn. www.rossportinn.on.ca

Thunder Bay

There are various little coves and inlets, villages and campsites as the road continues west (make sure you stop for the magnificent view of the cliffs at Ouimet Canyon Provincial Park – no campsites, picnic only) en route to Thunder Bay, the largest northern city in the Province of Ontario. Today's city was formed with the 1970 amalgamation of two cities – Port Arthur and Fort William – to become the third-largest port in Canada. It is the most westerly terminus for ocean-going vessels on the St Lawrence Seaway, as well as a centre for pulp-and-paper mills.

Highlights include exploring the Sleeping Giant Provincial Park, an island park just off the downtown harbour, a visit to Old Fort William that re-creates the fur-trading days of the North West Company's trading empire, the ski slopes in winter season, dinner at the Neebing Restaurant, and the good Finnish food and sauna at the 'Hoito'. (There are more people of Finnish descent in Thunder Bay than any other place in the world – except Finland.)

This is also a good location in which to rent a yacht or boat to explore the shoreline of Lake Superior.
Thunder Bay Tourism. Tel: (800) 667-8386; www.thunderbay.ca

Aquatic life at Quetico Provincial Park

Kakabeka Falls Provincial Park

Located just outside Thunder Bay, Kakabeka Falls is the centrepiece of Kakabeka Falls Provincial Park. This 38-m (125-ft) waterfall is an awesome sight in the middle of the wilderness – although a wilderness with a campsite, picnic facilities and visitor information.
www.ontarioparks.com/English/ kaka.html

Quetico Provincial Park

(*www.queticopark.com*) is en route to the international border towns of **Fort Frances** and **International Falls, Minnesota**, just across the bridge over Rainy River. Fort Frances is also a pulp-and-paper mill town and gateway to **Lake of the Woods** tourism.
www.ontarioparks.com/English/ quet.html

Kenora

This beautiful little northern town is the holiday heart of the Lake of the Woods region – an area filled with boating and sailing, fishing and hunting, swimming and hiking. Formerly known as Rat Portage, this little town of 10,000 also boasts its own symbol – a 13-m (43-ft) high muskie (a type of fish) made of wood, steel and fibreglass. Known as 'Husky the Muskie', the statue proudly honours one of the prize white fish catches of the area and the reasons thousands of fishermen descend on this pulp-and-paper mill town every year. This is the Cottage Country (*see p54*) area of the north, known for its clean waters, sailing regattas and little island homes in the middle of the lake.
Kenora Tourism. Tel: (807) 467-4637. www.kenora.ca

When to go

Because of the influence of the Great Lakes, the Province of Ontario experiences smaller variations in temperature and higher precipitation than would otherwise be expected for a region in the heart of a continent.

Southern Québec has a temperate climate, with four strongly contrasting seasons, including a short, mild spring and a colourful but often chilly autumn.

Ontario

In summer, the lakes have a cooling effect on neighbouring cities. However, in the south of the province, such as in Windsor or Toronto, heatwaves lasting up to a week, with temperatures higher than 30°C (86°F), are not uncommon.

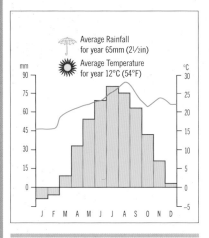

Average Rainfall
for year 65mm (2½in)

Average Temperature
for year 12°C (54°F)

WEATHER CONVERSION CHART

25.4mm = 1 inch
°F = 1.8 × °C + 32

In the autumn, the release of heat stored in the lakes has a moderating effect producing comfortable, sunny days and cool, bracing nights.

Winter is characterised by alternating currents of cold Arctic air and relatively warm air masses from the Gulf of Mexico. A city such as Sudbury, north of the Great Lakes, is obviously more subject to cold air currents and consequently has a more severe winter. In Toronto, a crisp day in January can easily sink to −20°C (−4°F).

Québec

Temperatures can exceed 30°C (86°C) in summer and drop below −25°C (−13°F) in winter.

There is snow on the ground for about 12 weeks in Montréal and up to 23 weeks in Gaspé. And, strangely enough, Montréal has more snow than such northern cities as Moscow and Oslo. In spite of this, Québec has more hours of winter sunshine than either Paris or London.

Québec City is glorious in sunny summer weather

Getting around

The best method of touring either province is by car – this provides the freedom to veer off the main highways and explore the little villages and towns scattered throughout both Ontario and Québec.

By car

Visitors are allowed to drive a vehicle for a maximum of six consecutive months without having an Ontario or Québec driving licence – as long as the driver possesses any other valid driving licence.

The speed limits and highway markers are posted in metric measurements and petrol is sold by the litre. For example, the speed limit in most cities or built-up areas is 50kmh (30mph) while the posted highway signs are 100kmh (60mph). Petrol will cost a driver about CDN$1 per litre.

Note that, in Québec, most road signs are written in French (since French is the only official language of the province), although international symbols accompany the written signage.

There are no right turns on red lights in the City of Montréal. You can turn right at every red light (unless specifically marked) in Ontario and Québec.

By public transport

Toronto and Montréal both boast an excellent transport system of trains, subways and buses that will connect you with any destination within that city. Both also have thousands of licensed taxis zooming around the vast metropolitan area.

There are no subways in Ottawa or Québec City, but you really don't need them in these smaller, more concentrated centres; both cities lend themselves to an urban walking experience. There are city buses, of course, but it is much easier to just hail a passing cab.

There is excellent and constant public transport along the busy traffic corridor between Windsor, Ontario to Québec City, Québec. This area is serviced by train and bus both day and night.

VIA Rail *(train). Tel: (888) 642-7245. www.viarail.ca (see also p12)*
Greyhound Canada *(bus). Tel: (800) 661-8747. www.greyhound.ca*

Accessibility issues

The guidelines are fairly uniform throughout both provinces and there are numerous signs denoting the level of assistance required for people with disabilities. Admission to tourist attractions is free for companions of persons with a disability.

Province of Ontario. *Ministry of Communiy and Social Services. Tel: (416) 789-4199. www.mcss.gov.on.ca*

Province of Québec. *Kéroul. Tel: (514) 252-3104. www.keroul.qc.ca*

Getting around

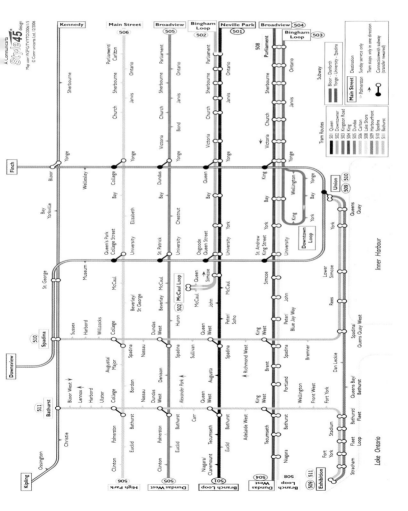

Accommodation

Both Anglo Ontario and francophone Québec provide any and every type of accommodation to suit your personal style, your family and your budget.

The tourist boards of each province and every major city have a plethora of booklets spanning every type of accommodation available, from ritzy, five-star suites (Four Seasons, Fairmont Hotels, Delta Hotels) to mid-range hotels (Holiday Inns) to cheap and cheerful one-star downtown lodgings, guesthouses, B&Bs and youth hostels. If you want to pay thousands of dollars for a hotel suite, no problem – you have a wide variety of hotels to choose from. However, it is still possible to get lodging in any major city of either province for less than $100 per night. Your travel agent can book accommodation for any star-rating, style, price range and location throughout both provinces. For stays of a week or more, you might want to consider 'apartment hotels' with full amenities that can be found in every major city.

Hotels

The major cities of Toronto, Ottawa, Montréal and Québec City are also major centres for trade shows and conventions, so each city is well equipped to handle any tourist enquiry regarding lodging.

The most recognisable hotels in Ontario and Québec are in Canada's Fairmont chain – Toronto's Royal York, Ottawa's Chateau Laurier, Montréal's Queen Elizabeth and Québec City's Chateau Frontenac. These are the massive, first-class, castle-like hotels built by the Canadian Pacific Railway in the early 19th century and owned by CP Hotels. When CP bought out the American Fairmont chain in 1999, they promptly changed their brand name to Fairmont in a shrewd marketing – if not patriotic – business decision. Another well-known chain is Toronto-born Four Seasons, now regarded as one of the premier hotel names in the world.

Resorts

Both provinces have huge rural recreational playground areas such as winter skiing and summer resorts. There re therefore literally thousands of hotels, motels, cottage rentals and widespread camping facilities to choose from.

For instance you can wine and dine in five-star splendour with your own luxury suite and spa facilities at Huntsville's Deerhurst Resort or the Québec wilderness at Fairmont's Le Château Montebello.

Campsites

Campsites and caravan parks are popular and plentiful; provincial and federal parks are always within short driving distances of wherever you end up. There are parks with complete amenities including electrical connections, hot showers, BBQs and restaurants, as well as wilderness camping, with just the loons for company.
Parks Canada. 25 Eddy Street, Gatineau, Québec. Tel: (888) 773-8888.
www.pc.gc.ca
Ontario Provincial Parks. Tel: (800) 668-2746. www.ontarioparks.com
Québec Provincial Parks. Tel: (877) 266-5687. www.bonjourquebec.com

Other accommodation choices

Roadside motels and lakeside cabins are ubiquitous in both provinces, along with big family resorts and hidden rustic cabins in the parks. Mobile home rentals and river houseboats are often booked months in advance, and every little town and village has good tourist information about the local guesthouses, B&Bs and friendly little motels located next to a good diner.

Winter weather depending, you can also book a night or two in Québec's famous Ice Hotel – all constructed and sculpted from nature's own ice and snow. But never fear – though the materials are cheap, the craftsmanship is excellent. It really isn't cold at all, and the experience is unforgettable.
R & R Houseboat Rentals. PO Box 275, Bridgenorth, Ontario.
Tel: (705) 793-8313.
www.rrhouseboats.com
Ice Hotel. 143, route Duchesnay Pavillion Regie, Sainte-Catherine-de-la-Jacques Cartier, Québec. Tel: (877) 505-0423 or (418) 875-4522.
www.icehotel-canada.com

For accommodation information:
Province of Ontario. *Tel: (800) ONTARIO (668-2746).*
www.ontariotravel.net

Province of Québec. *Tel: (877) BONJOUR (266-5687).*
www.bonjourquebec.com

Chateau Frontenac, Québec City

Accommodatioin

Food and drink

Canadian cuisine has never been defined as specifically as that of other countries around the world. When you mention Chinese, Japanese or Indian food, people can quickly conjure up some of their favourite dishes from those cultures. That is certainly not the case with Canadian cooking. Rather, various regions have always been known for producing specific culinary items – such as farm-raised beef and bison from the West, lobster and dulce from the Atlantic Provinces, fresh Atlantic salmon from the coast of British Columbia or venison from northern Ontario.

And then there are regional curiosities such as the indigenous poutine (*see p116*) from Québec. But Canadian cuisine has historically been a basic 'meat-and-potatoes' menu.

However, that started to change during the late 1960s, especially in the urban centres such as Toronto and Montréal, due to the influence of worldwide immigration to these cities. Suddenly new flavours and aromas were being added to the basically bland Canadian standard diet.

Then, in the 1980s, Canadian chefs discovered a national culinary pride and commenced creating their own signature dishes using the produce of the land – out went 'nouvelle cuisine' and in came new dishes of honey-cured venison, rich smoked salmon, salads with fiddleheads and wild mushrooms, desserts layered with the country's own maple syrup.

At the same time, Canada's wine industry started to receive international attention and glowing reports from wine aficionados everywhere. This new generation of chefs, combined with the burgeoning wine industry, was suddenly winning gold medals from international competitions: the country became known for more than maple syrup.

Many of these new Canadian culinary specialities started in Toronto. And because this is such a multicultural urban centre, it follows that there are more restaurants here that feature international cuisine than in any other city in the world.

Whatever your style – from Thai noodles to Cajun cornbread, Chinese dim sum to Hungarian goulash, delicate Japanese sushi to Jamaican jerk pork – you will find a restaurant catering to your taste buds somewhere in this city.

Québec, too, is a large multicultural centre, but the city has been known mainly for its fabulous French cuisine and late-night dinners in romantic candlelit restaurants – anywhere from a five-star restaurant in Montréal to a little country inn hidden away in the Charlevoix region. But most visitors (and residents) gravitate towards the famed delis of Montréal (Schwartz, The Main and Dunn's) where the cook piles smoked meats, barbecue ribs, chicken, fries and coleslaw onto huge platters as if they expect you won't be eating for the next two days.

And, of course, you cannot ignore the famous Montréal bagels.

The province's wine industry has always enjoyed the reputation of producing excellent wines to accompany either a deli sandwich or exquisite seven-course meals. In the dark days of nondescript cooking in Ontario, people would travel to Montréal or Québec City for a dining tour with a more exotic European touch.

Queen's Quay Terminal for shopping and dining, Toronto

Entertainment

Whatever your tastes in the vast world of entertainment, you will find a sample of everything in both provinces. In some cases, more than a sample; for instance, Toronto is the third-largest centre for theatre in the English-speaking world, right behind New York and London.

Performing arts, including opera, ballet, classical orchestras, dance, theatre, and so on, are in all the main cities in Ontario and Québec – Toronto, Ottawa, Montréal and Québec City, in particular, all have major performing arts centres and theatres.

Note that in Québec, of course, many of the theatres perform French-speaking productions and often the cinemas show only French-language films. Check the listings in the local newspapers for details.

The four major cities have a full range of nightlife and nightclubs, jazz bars and trendy lounges, fine dining and late-night bars. The definition of 'late night' changes with each province; in Ontario the last drink served is at 1.30am and the table will be cleared by 2am. In Québec, the time is more flexible and many places remain open until 4am.

Smokers in Ontario should be aware that this province – especially the City of Toronto – has one of the toughest anti-smoking bylaws in the world. You cannot light up in any building, including offices, shops, malls and definitely not restaurants or bars. Hence the people huddled together – even in mid-winter – on the public pavements puffing away before they return to their libations inside.

Sam's Record Shop, Toronto

Nightlife and eating out

Between the two provinces, you will find any and every type of cuisine, in establishments ranging from local pubs and diners to some of the world's best restaurants. The French have always led the way in Canada for culinary excellence (and the dining experience), but Ontario started to improve during the 1980s culinary revolution that saw the rise of the celebrity chef. Toronto, as the world's most multi-cultural city, can lay claim to the title 'city of world cuisine'.

Cinema and theatre

Toronto loves going to the movies; Montréal is not far behind. Both have huge film festivals every September. Theatre has also always been an integral part of both cultures. Québec, however, has developed its own unique brand of film and theatre *en français* that are distributed with subtitles or dubbed with English voices. Toronto and Ottawa are often home to stage musical productions from big name touring companies.

Cineplex (combined cinema chains of Famous Players and Cineplex Odeon). www.cineplex.com

Music, concerts and dance

All the major cities have a vast array of concert halls for both musical and dance performances, to accommodate both local performing arts organisations and international companies. However, the music and song of Québec is exceptional – from fiddling contests in the rural areas, to Francophone rock music in the Montréal Forum. The music of the Québeçois is unique and melodious but, with the exception of Celine Dion, unfortunately does not often soar beyond its borders.

A performance at the Stratford Festival

Shopping

The major cities of Ontario and Québec could be describe *as a shopper's paradise, with a vast array of retai* *opportunities. If you can't find it in Toronto, you probabl* *wouldn't want it anyhow, and shopping seems to be one o* *the favourite pastimes in Montréal.*

Goods & Services Tax (GST) refund

The GST is a 7 per cent federal tax (recently reduced from 8) that has been added to the tax in every province in the country.

Visitors may apply for a tax refund on the GST portion of the tax if the total amount of their purchases is at least $200 and the goods are taken out of Canada within 60 days. This applies to hotel and motel accommodation as well.

Pick up the form entitled *Tax Refund Application for Visitors* at any Canada Customs office at any airport or border crossing.

Once home, the visitor can send these itemised bills to: *Visitor Rebate Program, Revenue Canada, Summerside Tax Centre, Summerside, Prince Edward Island, Canada C1N 6C6. Tel: 1-800-66VISIT (1-800-668-4748).*

Duty-free shops

In Montréal, these include **AerRianta International** in the Saint-Laurent section of the island and **IGL Duty Free Shop** near the junction of Highways 15 and 87 near the New York border.

Canada Revenue Agency. *Tel: 1 (800) 668-4748. www.cra-arc.gc.ca/visitors*

Global Refund Canada. *Montréal Eaton Centre, 750 rue Sainte-Catherine Ouest. Tel: (514) 847-0982. www.globalrefund.com*

IGL Duty Free Shop. *Sainte-Bernard-de-Lacolle. Tel: (450) 246-2000. www.igldutyfree.com*

Premier Tax Free. *1166 rue Pierre-Mallet. Tel: (514) 633-1112. www.taxfree-services.ca*

Sales tax refund (Province of Québec)

Check for information on a refund of the 7.5 per cent provincial tax at various locations in Montréal (the airport, of course) and **Tourism Information Centres** (*1255 rue Peel*) but also at major department stores such as **Montréal Eaton Centre, Holt Renfrew and The Bay**.

ONTARIO

Niagara

What could be more Canadian than Niagara Falls? This is the land of souvenirs – some good, but most very, very tacky: just check out the souvenir shop at **Table Rock** for beaded belts that spell Canada across the back or Maple Leaf 'day-glo' key chains.

However, for some up-market and memorable souvenirs spend some time at **The Canada Shop** in nearby Jordan Village. This store specialises in authentic West Coast First Nations masks and jewellery, East Coast pewter, Inuit leather goods and sculptures and, of course, everything you could ever imagine in the way of maple syrup (tel: (905) 562-9714. www.thecanadastore.ca).

A better bet for authentic (and more expensive) shopping souvenirs can be found in the nearby **Niagara-on-the-Lake** which features some trendy boutiques filled with works by local artists and artisans, maple syrup in little bottles shaped like the Canadian maple leaf and handmade knits and woollen goods.

Ottawa

You will probably have the most fun shopping at the **ByWard Market** Square in the central core of Ottawa. You can buy groceries and food products, of course, but the shops and boutiques in one of the city's oldest buildings carry speciality items, works by local artists and crafts by First Nations artisans. For more convenient shopping, try the **Sparks Street Mall** (Canada's first pedestrian mall) just a block south of the Parliament Buildings, or the **Rideau Centre** which features some of the country's leading fashion retailers.

Toronto

Due to its vast and varied multicultural mix, you can find some unusual gifts and souvenirs scattered throughout this city, from the colourful saris in **Little India** (Gerrard Street East), trendy styles and funky stuff for the young along **Queen Street West**, practical winter coats and jackets in the jobber warehouses on **Spadina Avenue's Fashion District** and the chic and expensive purchases of **Bloor Street** (west of Yonge) and **Yorkville Avenue**.

The 'Mink Mile' of Bloor Street features brand names such as Harry Rosen, Chanel, Tiffany, Hermes and Eddie Bower (to name just a few) along with chic little boutiques. However, if you don't need a brand label on your purchases, just head down to the Fashion District and pick up that 'pretty-close-to-identical coat' for about a quarter of the price. In Toronto, the choice is yours.

The same bargain hunters browse through **Honest Eds**, a vast emporium of goods at Bloor and Bathurst – and even if you aren't planning to shop there, you must see it at night when the 22,000 flashing electric lights of the world's largest electric sign light up Bloor Street.

The two main downtown shopping centres are connected by underground tunnel and subway at Queen Street and Yonge – the **Eaton Centre** with more than 300 shops and restaurants starts at Dundas Street and runs south to the **Hudson's Bay Centre**. The Hudson's Bay Company (HBC) was founded in 1670 to supply furs and animal pelts to the British market, and is the oldest retailer in Canada.

For those who collect wines and spirits, take a trip to the **North Toronto Station** (Yonge Street at Summerhill) for a vast selection of more than 5,000 wines and spirits. This former railway station is now operated by the Liquor Control Board of Ontario (LCBO) and the qualified attendants will help you with your enquiries.

Shoppers will also need to peruse the distinctive Canadian fashions and designs in the **Queen's Quay Terminal** – a spacious shopping mall in an old converted shipping terminal.

The **Beach area**, Queen Street east of Woodbine, is also a fun and funky shopping street, a mix of trendy little boutiques and discount price shopping in between countless bars and restaurants. Check out **Ends** for bargain-basement discounts on designer labels at a fraction of the original price.

QUÉBEC
Montréal
You will find throngs of people wandering in and out of the thousands of stores and shops along **Ste Catherine Street** any day of the week.

Some of the shopping complexes along here include the **Montréal Eaton Centre**, **Complexe Desjardins**, **Complexe Les Ailes**, **La Foubourg Sainte-Catherine** and the **Promendae Cathédrale**. There are hundreds of shops, boutiques and galleries just in that little stretch alone.

More specialised gifts (such as Inuit sculpture and art) can be found in **Souvenirs Neil** in the Old Port as well as in the nearby **Canadian Maple Delights** that offers a complete array of maple syrup concoctions.

Smokers will want to visit the downtown speciality shop of **La Casa del Habano** with a complete array of cigars and pipe tobacco and a lounge to sit, read and relax over a fine cigar.

Montréal, city of museums, caters to consumers and souvenir hunters who are looking for the newest/oldest item that will highlight their Québec experience. In fact, many people do all their Christmas shopping in the numerous **museum boutiques** throughout the city. Reproductions of historical artefacts, wall paintings and archaeological curiosities can all be obtained from most of the museums including the Pointe-à-Callière (Museum of Archaeology and History), Montréal Biodôme, Musée d'art contemporain and, of course, everyone's favourite – the Montréal Insectarium.

Not only are Montréalers fashion-conscious but they are extremely aware

of the dangers facing our ecology as well. Which is why various '**eco shops**' have sprouted up all over the city, where bargain hunters search for both 'pre-loved' clothing and designer labels which they pack into their 'Atelier Scrap', which are bags made from recycled city banners.

Québec City

Billed as 'the most popular destination after Old Québec', the 350 stores in **place Laurier** claim the best in Canadian brand-name shopping as well as little speciality boutique shops and galleries. It will also get you into the Sainte-Foy area of Québec and show them there is a thriving modern city outside those old walls.

Eaton Centre, Toronto

There are certain streets in metropolitan Québec that locals flock to when they are in a consumer frenzy, specifically the **rue Garneau**, **place-Royale**, **rue Saint-Louis** and **rue Saint-Jean**. These streets offer shopping with a French flavour.

In particular, the 50 boutiques, art galleries and restaurants in the **Quartier Petit Champlain** have a distinct 17th-century feel since the shops are located in 400-year-old homes.

Rue Saint-Paul, in Québec's Lower Town, is frequented by antiques and art collectors who browse through the many galleries and boutiques. This is where any true collector will start a search for authentic Québecois works of art, paintings and crafts.

Collectors will also need to visit the

Musée d'art INUIT Brousseau (rue Saint-Louis) in the Old City. This Inuit art centre was founded in 1974 and contains the best selection of Inuit art and sculptures in the entire country.

Not everyone is an art collector, of course. For those who want an authentic yet affordable souvenir from this French province, pick up a cookery book of old Québecois recipes and try your hand at re-creating some of your favourite dishes when you return home. You can find cookery books in many stores, but it is recommended you visit **J A Moisan**, the oldest grocery store in North America (established in 1871) filled not only with food products but also with distinctive Québecois plate settings.

Sport and leisure

The Ontario and Québec residents of Canada are blessed with year-round sports and leisure activities – curling and skiing in the winter, swimming and sailing in the summer. Each province has some great slopes (especially the Mont Tremblant area in Québec) and countless lakes and rivers.

Golf

Ontario and Québec are replete with golf courses – both public and private – and many resorts (for example, Ontario's Deerhurst and Québec's Le Manoir Richelieu) have created their own professional courses. The courses closest to Toronto and Montréal can be quite crowded and very expensive. Get into the countryside, however, and both the prices and crowds decrease considerably.

Deerhurst Resort, 1235 Deerhurst Drive, Huntsville, Ontario.
Tel: (800) 441-1414. www.deerhurst.on.ca
Fairmont Le Manoir Richelieu, 181 rue Richelieu, La Malbaie, Charlevoix. Tel: (418) 665-3703. www.fairmont.com

Houseboating and sailing

Ontario and Québec were discovered through the trading routes of rivers and lakes. Those routes continue today, but the general public uses the vast water network for water sports from water skiing to canoeing. Many people holiday in rented houseboats to sail the canals and lakes while exploring the provinces, or take sailing lessons in the major cities or any little resort town on a body of water.

Professional franchise leagues

Toronto is actually one of the few cities in all of North America that can boast professional teams in four major sports – hockey, baseball, basketball and American football. Montréal, Ottawa and Québec City also have professional league sports and modern, state-of-the-art stadiums and arenas; these also serve as concert venues.

Provincial and Federal Parks

Both Ontario and Québec have developed superb amenities in hundreds of parks ranging from the massive Algonquin Provincial Park north of Toronto to the more rugged Forillon National Park in the Gaspé.
Many residents spend their annual holidays touring the parks, while

visitors often prefer to experience the provinces by camping in the Great Outdoors.

Skiing

Call it the luck of geography, but both provinces are blessed with great ski hills/mountains within an hour or two of the major population centres of Toronto, Ottawa, Montréal and Québec City. Mont Tremblant is the best known slope east of the Canadian Rockies, but the Collingwood area north of Toronto is just as popular.

The great outdoors

Residents and visitors can take full advantage of the wide-open spaces with a complete range of sports and leisure activities; camping and hiking, hunting and fishing, skiing and snowmobiling, sailing and houseboating, golf, tennis, snowboarding, skating, water skiing and ice fishing. In fact, during the winter the Rideau Canal in Ottawa freezes into the world's longest skating rink – many people who live close to the canal actually skate several miles to work every day.

Making the most of Ontario's lakes

Sport and leisure

Children

Both Ontario and Québec are very child-friendly, with the vast majority of hotels and motels providing family prices and discounts for children. There are family speciality attractions (from Toronto's Science Centre to Montréal's Olympic Park museums) and amusement theme parks (from Montréal's La Ronde to Toronto's Ontario Place) as well as world-class zoos (Toronto's Metro Zoo to Montréal's Granby Zoo) in the major cities of both provinces.

ONTARIO
Cottage Country
Santa's Village

It's Christmas minus the snow between June and Labour Day as kids spend the day as elves in a land of go-karting, mini-golf and laser tag.
Bracebridge, Muskoka. Tel: (705) 645-2512. www.santasvillage.ca

Niagara Falls
Marineland

One of the largest marine displays in the country (see p42).
8375 Stanley Avenue. Tel: (905) 356-9565. www.marineland.ca

Toronto
Centreville Amusement Park

A five-minute ferry ride from the Toronto harbourfront (see p38).
Toronto Islands. Tel: (416) 203-0405. www.torontoharbour.com. Open: May–Sept daily 10.30am–8pm. Family pass, adult and child tickets.

Ontario Place

Man-made islands just off Lakeshore Boulevard (see p30).
955 Lakeshore Boulevard West. Tel: (416) 314-9900. www.ontarioplace.com. Open: May–Sept daily 10am–midnight. Admission charge. Children's all-summer pass available.

Ontario Science Centre

This homage to science is a complete interactive, hands-on experience.
770 Don Mills Road. Tel: (416) 696-3127. www.ontariosciencecentre.ca

Paramount Canada's Wonderland

A day-long venture into the world of Hanna-Barbera cartoon characters, wet-water slide thrills, scary rides, a stage show and concerts.
9580 Jane Street. Tel: (905) 832-8131. www.canadas-wonderland.com. Open: May–Oct daily 9am–11pm. Day ticket or Season Pass.

Riverdale Farm

Right in the heart of Cabbagetown is a little park and petting zoo.
201 Winchester Street. Tel: (416) 392-6794. www.city.toronto.on.ca/parks/riverdalefarm.htm. Open: daily. Free admission.

Toronto Zoo

One of the world's premier zoos (*see p35*).
361 Old Finch Road. Tel: (416) 392-5900. www.torontozoo.com. Open: daily 9am–7pm. Admission charge.

Toronto environs
African Lion Safari

Just off the highway towards Hamilton your family can drive through a game reserve where lions, elephants and giraffes lope freely.
Safari Road (QEW highway, west of Toronto). Tel: (519) 623-2620. www.lionsafari.com

QUÉBEC
Montréal
The Haunted House

Poetry, terror, magic, dreams and fantasy all join hands to entertain you and your dinner guests in this spooky Victorian mansion. Montréal's Haunted House serves up a menu rich in terror and tasty theatrics.
1037 rue de Bleury. Tel: (514) 392-0004. www.maisonhantee.qc.ca. Open: June–Sept daily 10am–9pm. Reduced winter hours. Admission charge.

IMAX®TELUS Montréal Science Centre

The theatre features the latest and best of the IMAX® film productions (*see p87*).
King Edward Pier, Quays of the Old Port of Montréal. Corner of blvd Saint-Laurent and rue de la Commune. Tel: (514) 496-4629. www.montréalsciencecentre.com. Open: June–Sept daily 9am–10pm. Reduced hours in winter. Admission charge.

La Ronde

La Ronde amusement park offers more than 40 rides and attractions, plus dazzling shows (*see p89*).
Île Sainte-Hélène. Tel: (514) 397-2000. info@laronde.com. Open: May–Oct daily 10am–10pm. Admission charge (Season Pass). Two-ticket day package available.

Shed 16 Labyrinth

Located in a real shed, this labyrinth will drive you round the bend (*see p87*).
Clock Tower Pier, Quays of the Old Port of Montréal, Shed 16. Tel: (514) 499-0099. www.labyrintheduhangar16.com. Open: June–Sept daily 11am–9pm (weekends only from Oct–May). Admission charge.

TOHU, la Cité des arts du cirque

TOHU functions as both a creative and performance centre for the circus arts.
2345 rue Jarry Street Est. Tel: (514) 376-8648. www.tohu.ca. Open: June–Sept daily 10am–5pm (weekends only during school months). Admission charge.

Essentials

Canada has always prided itself on sharing the world's longest undefended border (6,420km/3,989 miles in length) with the United States. Due to recent world events, that may not be as true as it once was, but it is still the world's longest border between two countries, although it may take a little longer to cross these days.

Residents of the United States do not require a passport or a visa to enter Canada. However, they do require documents that establish citizenship, such as a birth certificate and at least one identification card with a photo.

Other nationalities should produce a valid passport and may require a visa depending on their country of origin. Residents of Britain, Ireland, Australia and New Zealand do not require a visa but should carry a valid passport.

(Note: officials may deny entry to anyone who has a criminal record, including convictions for driving while intoxicated.)

Canada has also introduced measures to reduce the possibility of child abduction. Children must have identification similar to the parents and/or a legal letter of permission for a child travelling with either one parent, relative or friend of the family.

Most items that you bring into Canada will be considered 'personal baggage' by Canada Customs.

You are allowed to bring in (tax free) a total of 200 cigarettes and 50 cigars (Cuban cigars are legal in Canada).

Visitors may also bring in up to 1.5 litres of wine tax free, 1.14 litres of liquor and up to 24 cans of beer. **Canada Border Services Agency.** *Calls from within Canada: (800) 461-9999. Calls from outside Canada: 1-204-983-3500 or 1-506-636-5064. www.cbsa-asfc.gc.ca* **Citizenship and Immigration Canada.** *www.cic.gc.ca*

Arriving/Entry formalities

You are not allowed to carry a weapon or bring firearms, especially handguns, into the country. There are certain exemptions for purposes of 'sport and hunting' as well as shooting competitions, but these must be confirmed in advance with **Canada Customs** (*Tel: (800) 959-2221*).

By air

Every province in Canada is readily accessible through international flights to every major city. Ontario has two main international airports, in Toronto and Ottawa, while Québec's major two international airports can be found in Montréal and Québec City.

Toronto's Pearson International Airport, with three busy terminals, is the largest airport in the country, while the smaller Ottawa Airport is well known by politicians and tourists alike as they fly into the nation's capital.

In Québec, the main terminal is Montréal Dorval Airport, the second being the province's capital city of Québec City.

These four airports are always busy, and transportation to and from each downtown core is constant with a steady stream of airport taxis, limos, shuttle buses and public transport.

By car

This is certainly the easiest way to cross the border for any citizen of the United States because every US state-issued licence is valid in Canada, both as a driver's licence as well as valid identification. Those from other countries should obtain an International Driver's Licence in advance. In addition, every driver on Canadian roads must show proof of vehicle registration and insurance coverage (these items are provided with all rental vehicles).

Drivers should note that seat-belt use is mandatory for all occupants of a vehicle anywhere in Canada. Also, leave any radar detection equipment at home; these machines are illegal in Ontario and Québec and may be confiscated by police.

The busiest border crossings into Ontario are the bridges between Detroit (Michigan) and Windsor, as well as the international bridges between Buffalo (New York) and/or Niagara Falls (New York) to Niagara Falls, Ontario.

The most popular border crossings into Québec are from New York state (Highway 87), Vermont (Highway 89) and New Hampshire (Highway 91) – these three routes range from 20km to 40km (12 miles to 24 miles) from the City of Montréal. The closest US crossing to Québec City (about 50km/31 miles) is along Highway 201 through the state of Maine.

By train

VIA Rail (*see p12*) is the country's passenger rail service and easily connects with the US-based AMTRAK Rail. The transition between countries is seamless and, since you are already on the train, the border check-in is

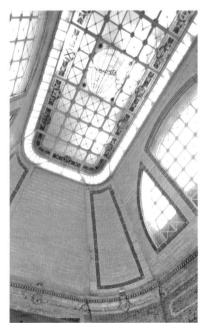

Québec City Station

much more pleasant. The most heavily travelled route is 'The corridor' running up from Windsor through Toronto, Montréal and Québec City. Contact VIA Rail for times and routes.

VIA Rail. *Tel: (888) 842-7245. www.viarail.ca*

By bus

Every Canadian city is connected by bus for the individual traveller and there are numerous coach companies that provide tours to every part of the country. Check with the central GreyHound Bus Information line for all local and national times and routes.

GreyHound Bus Terminal. *Tel: (800) 661-8747.*

By sea

There are international cruise ships that call on the Port of Québec City and Montréal, but most traffic along the St Lawrence Seaway and up into the Great Lakes consists of massive commercial freighters. However, there are many recreational sailors from the United States who cross the waters of the Great Lakes for quick weekend visits (they are required by law to enter at a harbour with a local Canada Customs office).

Car rentals

To rent a vehicle anywhere in Canada you must possess a valid driver's licence, photo identification and a recognised credit card – and be at least 25 years old. It is a good rule of thumb

(wherever you are in the world) to take a comprehensive insurance package on any rental vehicle. Ensure that you will not be liable for damages to yourself or any other person/vehicle as a result of a traffic accident.

The rules of the road follow the basic guidelines throughout North America. Those visiting from overseas should first and foremost remember one major rule – drive on the right-hand side of the road.

The maximum speed limits are usually 50km/h (31mph) in cities and 80km/h (50mph) on highways. On rural highways the posted speed limit may be 100km/h (62mph). Seat belts are mandatory.

Climate

Both provinces share similar weather patterns; very hot, sometimes steamy in the summer months (days of 30°C/86°F are not uncommon), balanced by winter months of snow, ice and cold (minus 20°C/minus 4°F). July is normally the hottest month, January the coldest. (Québec City often records the lowest temperatures of the major cities in Ontario and Québec.)

However, both provinces have a plethora of ski hills, some semi-mountains, many terrific winter resorts, lodges and auberges for winter getaways.

(Note: for a quick conversion to Fahrenheit, double the Celsius and add 32. For example: 20°C × 2 = 40 + 32 equals 72°F.)

Communications

To make an international call from Canada, dial *011* then the country code (Australia *61*, USA *1*, Ireland *353*, UK *44*), followed by the local code and the number.

Most places in Canada have run out of area codes due to the sudden proliferation of cell phone numbers; many urban centres now have three separate dialling codes (Toronto now uses *416*, *905* and *647*). The three numbers of the relevant dialling code must be dialled before the main number of seven digits. This is still only a local call, but you will have to dial all ten numbers.

All cell phones or mobile service (depending on your local carrier) should function the same in Canada as they do at home.

Electricity

Canada uses the standard North American 110-volt electrical power system (with two- or three-prong plugs). Overseas visitors who bring their own electrical equipment, from hairdryers to computers, will need an adaptor.

Goods & Services Tax (GST) refund

Known by Canadians coast-to-coast as the 'Gouge & Screw' Tax, the GST is a 7 per cent federal tax (recently reduced from 8) that has been added to the existing provincial tax (7 per cent in Ontario; 7.5 per cent in Québec). These two taxes appear at the bottom of every bill, including restaurant meals, hotels, car rentals, items of clothing, etc.

Visitors, however, may apply for a tax refund on the GST portion of the tax (*see p142*).

The province of Québec also allows for a rebate on provincial taxes on all goods and services – from hotel rooms and meals to souvenirs and clothing – purchased during your visit.
Contact: Tourisme Québec. PO Box 979, Montréal, Québec, Canada H3C 2W3. Tel: (800) 363-7777 or (514) 873-2015.

Hunting and fishing

Hunting and fishing laws in Canada are subject to the laws of each individual province. Anyone interested in these sports must contact the provincial authorities in Ontario and Québec for advance permission and licences.
Ontario: (800) ONTARIO (668-2746) or (416) 314-0944. www.mnr.gov.on.ca/fishing/oc.html. Québec: (800) 363-7777 or (514) 873-2015. www.gouv.qu.ca

In general, however, hunting is not permitted in national parks. Fishing in national parks may be allowed provided you obtain a special fishing licence.

Insurance

As a precaution, *every* visitor should take out personal travel health insurance before leaving on *every* trip. You should be adequately covered for any medical or health problems, the loss or theft of personal items, any type of personal liability or injury incurred while travelling in a foreign country.

Language

The two official languages – English and French – are enshrined in the Canadian Constitution as national working languages across the country. The Province of Québec, however, adopted an official policy in 1977 – under a Separatist Government – that made French the only official language of that province.

The majority of people in Ontario speak English (although in Toronto you will hear every language of the globe), while French is the predominant language in Québec. Fortunately, Québecers are much more adept than their Anglo counterparts at speaking both official languages, so a visitor will rarely have a problem with translation.

This is in the major cities, mind you; once you get into the Québec countryside you may have to get out your handy phrase booklets because many rural folk do not speak English. Fortunately again, Québecers (pronounced 'Kebekers') are very friendly and used to tourists so they will take the time to help you translate that menu. When in doubt, order 'steak frites' (steak and French fries) and the 'vin de la maison' (house wine). You can't go wrong (*see p156*).

Media

English-language publications are predominant and can also be found throughout the French-speaking province of Québec. The main newspaper written in French is *Le Devoir*, based in Montréal. The main English-language newspaper in Québec is *The Gazette*.

Toronto is one of the world's great cities for media and communications companies; this is also the only city in North America that publishes four daily newspapers seven days a week – *The Toronto Star*, *The Toronto Sun*, *The Globe & Mail* and *The National Post* (the latter two are distributed nationally).

Although there are additional publications in French throughout the Province of Québec, there are also publications in nearly every language in Toronto. This city has been declared 'the most ethnically diverse city in the world' and just about every nationality has its own newspaper, radio and television programming.

Metric

Canada uses the metric system of measurements.

Money matters

The currency system in Canada is based on dollars and cents – and loonies. The coins include a penny, nickel, dime, quarter, a 'loonie' and a 'twonie'. There are no single-dollar bills or two-dollar bills left in the country.

The first paper money is the $5 bill, then $10, $20, $50, $100 and so on.

The $1 coin, or loonie (so named for the Canadian loon on the one side) is gold in colour and slightly larger than a quarter. The $2 coin, or 'twonie', is two-toned – gold in the centre with a border of silver on the outside.

Like all world money markets, the exchange rate fluctuates on a daily basis. Check with any bank branch (there are exchange counters at every airport and in many hotels) as well as the local Thomas Cook or American Express offices in any urban centre.

All major brands of traveller's cheques and credit cards are accepted across Canada at every bank, hotel and store.

Most hotels and stores will change currency (especially US) into Canadian dollars but, as any traveller knows, the rate will be better at a recognised bank or financial institution.

Banking hours are general between 10am and 5pm, Monday to Friday, although bank machines for credit card transactions can be found on most street corners and convenience stores.

National holidays

1 January New Year's Day
March/April Good Friday
March/April Easter Sunday
March/April Easter Monday
24 May weekend Victoria Day
24 June St Jean Baptiste Day (QC)

Continued on p158.

Toronto currency

Language

Basic words and phrases

yes	oui	**behind**	derrière
no	non	**opposite**	en face de
please	s'il vous plaît	**right**	à droite
thank you	merci	**left**	à gauche
excuse me	excusez-moi	**straight on**	tout droit
I am sorry	pardon	**open**	ouvert
good morning	bonjour	**closed**	fermé
good evening	bonsoir	**hot**	chaud
good night	bonne nuit	**cold**	froid
goodbye	au revoir	**car**	voiture
the morning	le matin	**car park**	un parking
afternoon	l'après-midi	**petrol station**	un poste à essence
the evening	le soir	**parking**	stationnement
I have. . .	j'ai...	**prohibited**	interdit
It is. . .	c'est...	**bridge**	le pont
Do you speak		**street**	la rue
English?	Parlez-vous anglais?	**bus stop**	l'arrêt du bus
I do not		**underground**	
understand	Je ne comprends	**station**	la station de métro
when	pas	**railway station**	la gare
yesterday	quand	**platform**	le quai
today	hier	**bus station**	gare routière
tomorrow	aujourd'hui	**bakery**	boulangerie
at what time. .	demain	**supermarket**	supermarché
.?	à quelle heure. . .?	**bank**	banque
where is. . .?	où est. . .?	**toilets**	toilettes
here	ici	**post office**	PTT, poste
there	là	**stamps**	timbres
near	près	**chemist**	pharmacie
before	avant	**hospital**	hôpital
in front of	devant	**petrol**	essence

Numbers and quantity

one	un/une
two	deux
three	trois
four	quatre
five	cinq
six	six
seven	sept
eight	huit
nine	neuf
ten	dix
20	vingt
30	trente
40	quarante
50	cinquante
60	soixante
70	soixante-dix
80	quatre-vingts
90	quatre-vingt-dix
100	cent
1,000	mille
a little	un peu
enough	assez
much/many	beaucoup
too much/many	trop

Days of the week

Monday	lundi
Tuesday	mardi
Wednesday	mercredi
Thursday	jeudi
Friday	vendredi
Saturday	samedi
Sunday	dimanche

Months

January	janvier
February	février
March	mars
April	avril
May	mai
June	juin
July	juillet
August	août
September	septembre
October	octobre
November	novembre
December	décembre

1 July Canada Day
1st weekend August civic holiday
1st weekend September Labour Day
2nd Monday October Canadian Thanksgiving
11 November Remembrance Day (government offices and banks close)
25 December Christmas Day
26 December Boxing Day

Passports and visas

Entry into Canada and the United States differs according to your country of origin. Most Canadian and US citizens may cross the Canada–US border provided they have proof of citizenship with them: a birth certificate or a certificate of naturalisation (note that a driver's licence does not quality as proof), although it is recommended that you bring your passport. Other nationalities should check with the Canadian embassy before travelling.

Places of worship

Canada has a full range of churches, temples, mosques, synagogues, etc. for

Post Office building in Ottawa

every religious order, group or belief throughout the world. The French-based province of Québec has a higher percentage of Catholic cathedrals than the English-Scottish background of its Ontario neighbours.

Post offices

The days of the official post office ended during the mid-1990s all across Canada. Most official federal post office buildings are closed to the public and used only for handling and sorting. The services of the post office have been handed over to the local grocery store, convenience shop, pharmacy or print shop. You will find a post office symbol outside the various locations. Stamps are available in just about any corner or variety store. Sending a basic envelope anywhere in Canada now costs 52 cents, a letter to the US costs 65 cents and it's $1.69 for an overseas envelope.

Public phones

In this day and age of cell (mobile) phones and text messaging, public telephones – once found everywhere – have been slowly disappearing from the street corners. They are operated with either coins or phone cards. If you are making an international call with a phone card, dial *800* to get the operator then follow the instructions. However, if you are suddenly in need of a phone, the majority of store owners will let you use their phone for a local call, or just ask anyone with a mobile phone.

Smoking

The Province of Ontario – especially the capital city of Toronto – has led the charge and banned smoking in all public places and spaces including offices, malls and shops. The complete ban also applies to restaurants and – to the chagrin of smokers – all bars as well. In fact, Toronto was the first city in North America to introduce these strict measures.

Time zones

Since Canada is the second-largest country in the world (after Russia), it stretches to include six different time zones. Ontario and Québec are both included in the Eastern Time Zone (GMT –5 hours, the same as New York), so you won't have to change your watch when you cross the border into either province.

Tipping

This has become a standard way of life for Canadians, and a necessary one for others. The average tip for a restaurant meal is 15 per cent of the bill. It is expected that people will normally leave a tip in a bar for their server or bartender. Hotel cleaning staff should receive $5 per day and bellhops usually get $2 per bag. Hairdressers and barbers usually receive between 10 and 20 per cent – depending how you look afterwards.

Emergencies

Emergency services

Dial 911 for emergency services (police, fire, ambulance) from any location in Canada. It's a free call, even from a payphone.

Crime

Canada remains one of the acknowledged low-crime countries in the world. (Note: handguns are illegal.) The two largest cities, Toronto and Montréal, have the lowest crime rate per capita of any city in the world; Ottawa and Québec City have slightly higher rates. Of course, it is not utopia and, like any urban centre, there are always certain areas that are less desirable to explore than others. Your concierge or any employee of the city's transit system will assist you with your excursions.

US Embassy in Ottawa

Drugs

All street drugs remain illegal in Canada. If you are caught with them, you will be arrested, charged and, if found guilty, expelled from the country and forbidden from entering Canada again.

Prescription drugs should be clearly marked; if possible, bring a supporting document from your doctor. Also, make sure you have a copy of your prescription in case you require a refill from a doctor in Canada.

Health

There are no special inoculations or vaccinations required for entering Canada unless there is an international health warning pertaining to the area you are arriving from. Canada has never been known for any tropical diseases.

Canada's health-care system is funded by the province or territory, and almost all Canadians qualify for coverage. Any visitors should have a health plan from their country of origin, although most travellers today take out travel insurance for the duration of their visit.

Embassies and consulates

Australia. 50 O'Connor Street, Suite 710, Ottawa, Ontario K1P 6L2. *Tel: (613) 236-0841.*
Ireland. 130 Albert Street. Suite 1105, Ottawa, Ontario K1P 5G4. *Tel: (613) 233-6281.*

New Zealand. 99 Bank Street. Suite 727, Ottawa, Ontario K1P 6G3. *Tel: (613) 238-6097.*
South Africa. 15 Sussex Drive, Ottawa, Ontario K1M 1M8. *Tel: (613) 744-0330.*
UK. 80 Elgin Street, Ottawa, Ontario K1P 5K7. *Tel: (613) 237-1530.*
USA. 490 Sussex Drive, Ottawa, Ontario K1N 1G8. *Tel: (613) 238-5335.*

Canadian embassies abroad

Australia. Canadian High Commission. Commonwealth Avenue, Canberra ACT 2600, Australia. *Tel: 61 (2) 6270-4000 (also in Melbourne, Perth and Sydney).*
New Zealand. Canadian High Commission. 3rd floor, 61 Molesworth Street, Thorndon, Wellington, New Zealand. *Tel: 64 (4) 473-9577.*
South Africa. 60 St George's Mall, Cape Town 8001. *Tel: 27 (21) 423-5240.*

UK. Canadian High Commission. Canada House, Trafalgar Square, London SW1Y 5BJ, England. *Tel: 44 (20) 7258-6600 (also in Belfast, Birmingham, Cardiff, Edinburgh).*

USA. Canadian Consulate General. 16th floor, Exxon Building, 1251 Avenue of the Americas, New York, NY 10020-1175. *Tel: (212) 596-1600*; 9th floor, 550 South Hope Street, Los Angeles, CA 90071-2627. *Tel (213) 346-2700 (also in Atlanta, Boston, Buffalo, Chicago, Dallas, Detroit, Honolulu (Hawaii), Miami, Minneapolis, San Juan (Puerto Rico) Seattle, Washington).*

Directory

Accommodation price guide

For the accommodation listings in this directory,
a star rating indicates the price range.
Prices are per room per night.

★	under $100
★★	under $200
★★★	over $200

Eating out price guide

The star system below is based on the average price of
a meal for one person without drinks or tips.

★	under £25
★★	under £50
★★★	over £100

PROVINCE OF ONTARIO

Muskokas

ACCOMMODATION

Algonquin Park ★
Reserve one of the 1,248 pitches in eight public campsites (especially on long summer weekends) or paddle to wilderness areas along numerous canoe routes.
Box 248, Whitney.
Tel: (705) 633-5661.
www.algonquinpark.on.ca

Arowhon Pines ★★
Relax in the resort's huge chalet-type cabins – private bedrooms with a common living room with stone fireplace. Meals are served in the main lodge. (Note: Avoid blackfly season in June!)
Box 10001, Algonquin Park, Huntsville.
Tel: (705) 633-5661 (summer);
297 Balliol Street, Toronto M4S 1C7. Tel: (416) 483-4429 (winter).
www.arowhonpines.ca

Deerhurst Resort ★★★
Long known as Ontario's premier resort, this four-season property on Peninsula Lake contains several championship golf courses, tennis courts, saunas, spas, fine dining and accommodation ranging from chalets to time-share condos.
1235 Deerhurst Drive, Huntsville.
Tel: (800) 441-1414.
www.deerhurst.on.ca

EATING OUT

Muskokas

Weber's ★
This hamburger/French fries/milkshake pit stop is so popular the restaurant built a bridge across the highway to service customers heading to and from their weekend cottages.
Highway 11, north of Orillia.
Tel: (705) 325-3696. www.webersrestaurants.com

Simcoe County

Restaurant ★★
This cosy – and popular – European-style restaurant is the brainchild of chef Doug Porter who uses local producers to conjure up his own original organic creations for residents of Cottage Country.
206 Hurontario Street, Collingwood.
Tel: (705) 445-6957.
www.simcoecountyrestaurant.ca

Deerhurst Resort ★★★
The most exclusive resort in Cottage Country also serves some of the best meals in its many restaurants, including fine dining with candlelight and wine as well as more casual bars and pubs.
1235 Deerhurst Drive, Huntsville.
Tel: (800) 441-1414.
www.deerhurst.on.ca

Niagara Falls
ACCOMMODATION
Casino Hotels ★★–★★★
There are four major hotels in the middle of the Niagara strip, opposite the American Falls, and directly connected to Casino Niagara:
Brock Plaza
Falls
Skyline Inn
Hampton Inn at the Sheraton on the Falls
Tel: (800) 263-7135. www. NiagaraFallsHotels.com
Great Wolf Lodge ★★
A perfect family holiday spot complete with gigantic indoor waterpark (13 water slides), 18-hole outdoor mini-golf course and five family-themed restaurants all centred

around a 406-suite resort.
3950 Victoria Avenue.
Tel (800) 605-9653.
www.greatwolflodge.com
Travelodge Clifton Hill ★
This is the closest motel to the Falls. Located right in the heart of Clifton Hill, a guest can simply leave the car and walk to the Casino, the Falls and most major attractions from this location.
4943 Clifton Hill.
Tel: (866) 656-0309.
www.falls.com

Niagara-on-the-Lake
ACCOMMODATION
The Angel Inn ★
This elegant old inn features comfortable colonial-style guest rooms and suites, a friendly pub and fine dining. And if you are fortunate, you might see a spectral figure or two during the night.
224 Regent Street.
Tel: (905) 468-3411.
www.angel-inn.com
The Oban Inn ★★
The village's original charming 25-guest room country inn right beside the golf course with a

magnificent view of the lake and glassed-in porch for dining.
160 Front Street.
Tel: (888) 669-5566 or (905) 468-2165.
www.obaninn.com
The Prince of Wales Hotel & Spa ★★★
Deluxe accommodation, fine dining and spa facilities just opposite the old clock standing in the middle of town.
6 Picton Street.
Tel: (888) 669-5566 or (905) 468-3246.
www.vintageinns.com

EATING OUT
The Buttery ★
Serving wenches in period costume bring in big bowls of homemade soup and hearty sandwiches for a pre-theatre lunch.
19 Queen Street.
Tel: (905) 468-2564.
www.thebuttery.ca
The Prince of Wales Hotel & Spa ★★★
This grand hotel, only two blocks from any theatre at the Shaw, also serves an excellent pre-matinee lunch and sumptuous après-theatre buffet.
6 Picton Street.
Tel: (888) 669-5566 or

(905) 468-3246.
www.vintageinns.com

Ottawa

ACCOMMODATION

**Delta Ottawa Hotel &
Suites ★★–★★★**
Luxury suites at
affordable prices right in
the heart of Ottawa's
busy shopping areas and
a brief stroll to the
parliament buildings.
361 Queen Street.
Tel: (613) 238-6000).
www.deltahotels.com

**Fairmont Château
Laurier ★★–★★★**
Another of Canada's
original 'railway hotel'
castles is a favourite with
all tourists and
politicians visiting the
nation's capital.
1 Rideau Street.
Tel: (613) 236-5000.
www.fairmont.com

EATING OUT

**Friday's Roast Beef
House ★**
Roast prime rib, steaks
and seafood served in one
of the city's heritage
buildings. Entertainment
and late-night menu in
the upstairs piano lounge.
150 Elgin Street.
Tel: (613) 237-5353.

Luxe Bistro ★
Conveniently located in
the ByWard Market, this
24-hour bistro serves a
generous steak frites with
an excellent selection
of wines.
47 York Street.
Tel: (613) 241-8805.
www.luxebistro.com

Le French Quarter ★★★
Across the river in
Gatineau, this restaurant
serves lobster, oysters and
shrimp tinged with New
Orleans-style flavours.
Patios overlooking the
Ottawa skyline as well as
private dining rooms.
80 Promenade du Portage.
Tel: (819) 777-1125.

Port Dover

ACCOMMODATION

The Brant Hill Inn ★
Book early for one of the
comfortable four-poster
beds in this 14-room inn
overlooking the harbour
just up the hill past the
Lift Bridge.
*30 John Street. Tel: (519)
583-1501. www.
branthillinnandspa.com*

The Erie Beach Hotel ★
Just steps from the
boardwalk, this urban
motel features good basic
accommodation right in

the middle of the Port
Dover Beach action.
19 Walker Street.
Tel: (519) 583-1391.
www.eriebeachhotel.com

EATING OUT

Erie Beach Hotel ★★
Perfect perch pan-fried
in breadcrumbs, shrimps
and scallops, baskets of
fries and celery bread
provide a feast.
19 Walker Avenue.
Tel: (519) 583-0880.
www.eriebeachhotel.com

**Imaginations Fine
Food ★**
This is the place to stock
up on chef Anthony's
creative cuisine,
marinated meats for the
barbecue and huge deli
sandwiches.
301 Main Street.
Tel: (519) 583-9195.
*www.imaginationsfine
foods.com*

Point Pelee

EATING OUT

**Pelee Island Winery
Pavilion ★**
Don't miss the experience
of dining al fresco on this
little island; savour the
olives and cheeses, along
with the barbecue
burgers and chicken, with

various Pelee island wines. The local winery rep will guide you on the best choice of wine for those barbecue ribs.
Pelee Island.
Tel: (519) 733-6551.
www.peleeisland.com

Port Stanley
ACCOMMODATION
Inn on the Harbour ★
This cosy country inn mirrors the décor of The Port with a warm nautical feel and hearty seafaring food.
202 Main Street.
Tel (519) 782-7623.
www.innontheharbour.ca

EATING OUT
Kettle Creek Inn ★
Fish is the featured item on this menu as the comfortable dining room highlights the village's long-time fishing industry.
216 Joseph Street.
Tel: (519) 782-3388.
www.kettlecreekinn.com

Stratford
ACCOMMODATION
Bentley's Inn ★–★★
This downtown inn features luxury two-level suites just a few minutes'

walk from the various theatres, restaurants and shops.
99 Ontario Street.
Tel: (519) 272-1853 or (800) 362-5322.
www.bentleys-annex.com
Victorian Inn on the Park ★
This 115-unit motel is located at the edge of the park within a ten-minute stroll along the Avon River to the main Festival Theatre. There is an 18-hole golf course right across the street.
10 Romeo Street.
Tel: (519) 271-4650 or (800) 741-2135.
www.victorian-inn.on.ca
The Queen's Inn at Stratford ★–★★
A completely renovated 32-room inn, circa 1850, with delightful spacious rooms and suites, and fine dining at Henry's.
161 Ontario Street.
Tel: (519) 271-7373 or (800) 461 6450. www.queensinnstratford.com

EATING OUT
The Boar's Head Pub ★
Casual olde-English-style pub with weekend entertainment, an outdoor

patio and huge breakfasts commencing at 7am. Companion to the more upmarket Henry's Dining Room.
Queen's Inn, 161 Ontario Street. Tel: (519) 271-1400. www.queensinnstratford.ca
Rundles Restaurant ★★★
Always makes every top list for the best in Canada. The restaurant overlooks the beautiful park and Avon River but you may not notice any of that when the culinary treats reach the table. For something special, try the pan-roasted rack of Ontario venison.
9 Cobourg Street.
Tel: (519) 271-6442. www.rundlesrestaurant.com
The Church ★★★
This really is an old church and you would be forgiven for calling the food divine. The pews have been removed for dining under the cathedral ceiling or upstairs in the more casual Belfry.
70 Brunswick Avenue.
Tel: (519) 273-3424.
www.churchrestaurant.com

Toronto

ACCOMMODATION

Fairmont Royal York ★★–★★★

Canada's CP Hotels & Resorts purchased the Fairmont chain then adopted that name for brand recognition. This 1,400-room grand dowager hotel towers over Front Street and Union Station.
100 Front Street West.
Tel: (416) 368-2511.
www.fairmont.com

The Four Seasons/ Yorkville ★★★

One of the top luxury hotel chains in the world has its flagship hotel (with film star clientele) on the corner of trendy Yorkville Avenue complete with excellent credit card dining.
21 Avenue Road.
Tel: (416) 964-0411.
www.fourseasons.com

Holiday Inn on King ★★

Located in the heart of the downtown Entertainment District, this medium-priced hotel is perfectly located for a weekend of theatre, concert halls and sports stadiums.
370 King Street West.
Tel: (416) 599-4000.
www.hiexpress.com/ torontodtwn

EATING OUT

Stratengers ★

The thin-crust pizza (cooked in a wood-fired oven), huge burger platters and superb Indian food combined with low, low prices make this the best restaurant in town.
130 Queen Street East.
Tel: (416) 466-8934.
www.stratengers.com

Jamie Kennedy Wine Bar ★★★

A casual and relaxed atmosphere where you can purchase wines of international reputation by the glass and small servings of Jamie Kennedy's culinary specialities. In this case, the food enhances the taste of the wine.
9 Church Street.
Tel: (416) 362-1957.
www.jkkitchens.com

Susur ★★★

Hailed as one of the most creative chefs in North America, Susur Lee's name guarantees a sell-out every night as diners delight in his inventive infusions of Asian and Western cooking. Bring money.
601 King Street West.
Tel: (416) 603-2205.
www.susur.com

ENTERTAINMENT

Toronto is known as the Entertainment Capital of Canada for its plethora of new and restored theatres, music and concert halls as well as the two downtown state-of-the-arts sports stadiums. Not only that, but the city's reputation as 'Hollywood North' is well deserved for the number of films and television programmes filmed in and around its streets – it is rare not to see dozens of huge equipment trucks parked all over town.
Note: The main ticket outlets for theatres, concerts and entertainment are TicketMaster (www.ticketmaster.ca) and TicketKing (www.ticketking.ca).

Buddies in Bad Times Theatre

This downtown theatre produces both gay and lesbian themed plays that highlight both the drama nd comedy of alternative lifestyles. *12 Alexander Street, East of Yonge. Tel: (416) 975-8555. www.buddiesinbadtimes theatre.com*

Canon Theatre
This 2,265-seat vaudeville-era theatre was saved from the wrecker's ball to become one of the city's most popular venues for large-scale productions. The entrance is actually on Yonge Street across from the Eaton Centre. *244 Victoria Street, East of Yonge. Tel: (416) 364-4100. www.canontheatre.com*

Elgin Theatre/Winter Garden
The Ontario government discovered a long-forgotten theatre (the 991-seat Winter Garden) sitting on top of the boarded up 1,563-seat Elgin. A $28 million renovation has restored these two 1913 stages to their golden glory. *189 Yonge Street, South of Dundas. Tel: (416) 872-5555.*

The Four Seasons Centre for the Performing Arts
Opened in late 2006, this arts centre is now home to the Canadian Opera Company and National Ballet of Canada. The horseshoe-shaped, five-tiered, 2,144-seat auditorium has already been hailed as one of the world's great halls. *145 Queen Street West (at University). Canadian Opera Company. Tel: (416) 363-8231). National Ballet of Canada. Tel: (416) 345-9686. www.fourseasonscentre.ca*

Glenn Gould Studio
The perfect little concert/recording studio often used by the CBC for live radio performances and recorded concerts. Book your tickets early for this intimate 341-seat theatre. *CBC Broadcast Centre, 250 Front Street West. Tel: (416) 205-5555.*

The Hummingbird Centre for the Performing Arts
Another large venue (3,155 seats) used by touring productions and special entertainment acts from Broadway's famed Rockettes to Las Vegas magician David Copperfield. *1 Front Street at Yonge. Tel: (416) 872-2262.*

Massey Hall
The stately Victorian-era stage (2,715 capacity) is always a favourite venue for both performers and audiences; Canada's folk troubadour Gordon Lightfoot plays only Massey for his annual sold-out, four-evening concerts. *178 Victoria Street, East of Yonge. Tel: (416) 872-4255. www.masseyhall.ca*

Molson Amphitheatre
One of the city's great lakeside concert venues (summer only) that features touring musical performers ranging from Jimmy Buffett to Bob Seger. *Ontario Place, 955 Lakeshore Blvd. Tel: (416) 870-8000.*

Princess of Wales Theatre
The first (and quite spectacular) theatre to be built in North America in the past 40 years (with private funds from Ed and David Mirvish) was

designed to showcase grand-scale Broadway plays in this 2,000-capacity venue.
300 King Street West. Tel: (416) 872-1212. www.mirvish.ca

Roy Thomson Hall

The home of the Toronto Symphony Orchestra, this stunning 2,812-seat concert hall also plays host to many touring musical acts from classical performances to stars of Broadway.
60 Simcoe Street, South of King Street West. Tel: (416) 593-4828. www.roythomson.ca

Royal Alexandra Theatre

The stately old grande dame of Toronto's theatre scene (1,500 seats) welcomes touring productions from Broadway and London's West End as well as highlighting new Canadian works.
260 King Street West. Tel: (416) 872-1212. www.mirvish.ca

St Lawrence Centre for the Arts

Two theatres under one roof, both with fewer than 1,000 seats, make this an intimate venue for theatre, often introducing new and/or original Canadian plays.
27 Front Street, East of Yonge. Tel: (416) 366-7723. www.stlc.ca

SPORTS STADIUMS/ ENTERTAINMENT VENUES

The main ticket outlet for sporting events and touring concerts is TicketMaster (*www.ticketmaster.ca*).

Air Canada Centre (ACC)

Now home to two professional sports franchises – Toronto Maple Leafs hockey and Toronto Raptors basketball – the new $260-million ACC is centrally (and perfectly) located directly behind Union Station on Front Street just west of Yonge. The 21,000-seat arena easily converts into a concert hall for big-name touring acts from Elton John to Bruce Springsteen.
40 Bay Street, South of Front Street West. Tel: (416) 872-5000 (sports), (416) 870-8000 (concerts). www. theaircanadacentre.com

The Rogers Centre (formerly The SkyDome)

Toronto is the only city in North America that has two major sports stadiums just two blocks from each other in the thriving downtown business centre. The Toronto Blue Jays (baseball) and Toronto Argonauts (football) claim this dome as their home turf. The 67,000-seat arena conveniently converts to a huge concert stadium for large touring musical performances. It is still impressive to watch the world's first retractable dome slowly open during a sunny day in the baseball season.
1 Blue Jays Way, South of Front Street West. Tel: (416) 341-1234. www.rogerscentre.com

PROVINCE OF QUÉBEC
ACCOMMODATION
Charlevoix
Auberge des Peupliers ★

Basic, unpretentious accommodation in the heart of the Charlevoix region – with one of the

...est kitchens in the province.

381 rue Saint-Raphael, Cap-à-l'Aigle. Tel: (418) 665-4423. www. aubergedespeupliers.com

Fairmont Le Manoir Richelieu ★★–★★★

This legendary railway hotel, located in the rural countryside, recently underwent a $140-million renovation complete with spa, casino and golf course.

181 Rue Richelieu, La Malbaie. Tel: (418) 665-3703. www.fairmont.com

EATING OUT

Le Rustique/Resto Pub ★

This little unpretentious restaurant/pub in the middle of Baie-St-Paul serves a delicious, inexpensive five-course steak frites. Take a lunch break here from your art gallery excursions.

10 rue Forget, Baie-St-Paul. Tel: (418) 435-5016.

Auberge des Peupliers ★★★

This unassuming country inn creates one of the most memorable meals you will ever experience; try the rack of lamb and a foie gras that literally

melts in your mouth.

381 rue Saint-Raphael, Cap-à-l'Aigle. Tel: (418) 665-4423. www. aubergedespeupliers.com

Auberge la Coudière ★★

A taste treat featuring Charlevoix regional cuisines as well as specialities from throughout the province, all with produce from local farms in the region.

2891 chemin de la Baleine, Île-aux-Coudres. Tel: (418) 438-2838 or toll free (888) 438-2882. www. aubergelacoudiere.com

Gaspé

ACCOMMODATION

Îles de la Madeleine Château Madelinot ★

A large, hospitable 120-room combination hotel/motel with a kitchen prepared to pack a picnic lunch for your excursions along the cliffs of Île du Cap aux Meules.

323 Fatima. Tel: (418) 969-4073. www. islesdelamadeleine.com/ hotels

Les Petites Maisons du Parc ★

Alpine-style cottages, with up to four

bedrooms, overlooking the spectacular sunrise over the Baie of Gaspé.

910 boulevard Forillon. Tel: (418) 892-5873. www.gesmat.ca

EATING OUT

Bistro-Resto Le Brise Brise ★★

Fish and seafood specialities from the grill as well as a complete international menu. Member of the Gaspésie Goumande.

135 rue de la Reine. Tel: (418) 368-1456. www.brisebrise.com

Sainte-Anne-des-Monts ★★

Fine Québec cuisine including fresh game, fish and seafood. Café and bistro menu as well, plus the restaurant will prepare packed lunches.

2001 route du Parc. Tel: (418) 763-3321. www.riotel.com

Îles de la Madeleine

EATING OUT

Auberge La Maree Haute ★★

Specialising in some of the freshest seafood and fish you will ever taste. What else would you expect from a restaurant in the middle of the ocean.

25 chemin des Fumoirs (Havre-Aubert).
Tel: (418) 937-2492.
www.ilesdelamadeleine/ mareehaute

La Maison d'Eva-Anne ★★

Creative meals made from local produce including clam chowder, beer cod patties and homemade breads.

326 chemin de la Pointe-Basse (Havre aux Maisons).
Tel: (418) 969-4053.
www.grandlarge.ca

Laurentians

ACCOMMODATION

Club Tremblant l'Hotel du Lac ★★

One of the closest lodges/resorts with full amenities right beside the slopes of Mont Tremblant.

121 rue Cuttle.
Tel: (819) 425-8781.
www.hoteldulac.ca

EATING OUT

Val-David ★

Casual and relaxed country buffet style with regional dishes and maple ham along with a deli counter and dancing in the evening.

1030 route 117 (Mont Tremblant).
Tel: (819) 322-2246.
www.valdavid.com

Le Cheval de Jade ★★

Fine Québecois cuisine and regional food products with specialities including bouillabaisse, seafood and duck.

688 rue de Saint-Jovite (Mont Tremblant).
Tel: (819) 425-5233.
www.chevaldejade.com

Montréal

ACCOMMODATION

Fairmont Queen Elizabeth ★★–★★★

Conveniently located in the heart of Montréal right over the main railway station with connecting subway lines.

900 boulevard Rene-Levesque Ouest. Tel: (514) 861-3511.
www.fairmont.com

Hotel XIX siècle ★★–★★★

Old-fashioned relaxed luxury and personal service in the heart of Old Montréal in this intimate yet spacious 58-room hotel.

262 rue Saint-Jacques.
Tel: (514) 985-0019.
www.hotelxixsiecle.com

'Le Beau Soleil' in Old Montréal ★★

A lovely yet very affordable five-bedroom B&B near the romantic Old Port walkway.

355 rue St Paul Street Est.
Tel: (514) 871-0299.
www.aubergebonsecours

EATING OUT

Schwartz Deli ★

The king of all delis. Montréalers swear by this unpretentious little hole-in-the-wall and queue patiently for their platters of smoked meats, brisket and borscht.

3895 boulevard Saint-Laurent.
Tel: (514) 842-4813.
www.schwartzdeli.com

Restaurant Europea ★★

An exceptional combination of style and cuisine (try the lobster cappuccino) with a blend of chic décor and surprisingly reasonable prices. Not to be missed.

1227 rue de la Montagne.
Tel: (514) 398-9229.
www.euoropa.ca

Restaurant du Vieux Port ★★

Live lobsters, fresh seafood and Alberta AAA beef served in the marine atmosphere of this classic restaurant in the old city. *39 rue St-Paul Est. Tel: (514) 866-3175. www. restaurantduvieuxport.com*

Le Cabaret du Roy – Restaurant ★★★
Period musicians, historic figures and an Old World table. Amerindian dishes, locally grown Québec produce and grilled game add authentic flavour to the feasting and festivities. *363 rue de la Commune Est. Tel: (514) 907-9000. www.oyez.ca*

Entertainment

There are numerous entertainment venues, theatres and concert halls throughout this vibrant city. Many productions, however, are only *en français*. If you are fortunate, you will be able to catch a revival of David Fennario's classical play *Balconville*, the first bilingual Canadian theatrical presentation which also provides an insider's look at modern life in bilingual Montréal. The most popular ticket agency is the website for the Place des Arts: *www.billetterie.pda.qc.ca*

The CinéRobothèque
The CinéRobothèque is the National Film Board's high-tech centre. It offers unique technology: a robot, like a jukebox, plays movies selected from a collection of more than 8,000 titles. Users can access 65 years of Canadian experience through documentaries, animated shorts and feature films. *1564 rue Saint-Denis. Tel: (514) 496-6887. www. nfb.ca/cinerobotheque*

Les Grands Ballets Canadiens de Montréal
Les Grand Ballets performs a wide repertory of classics and modern works while also inviting prestigious international ballet companies each year to Place des Arts. *260 boulevard de Maisonneuve. Tel: (514) 849-8681. www.grandsballets.com*

Opéra de Montréal
The Opéra, founded in 1980, ranks among North America's 15 top opera companies with over 70,000 spectators attending its productions

each year. To date, the company has staged more than 800 performances of 87 different operas. *286 boulevard de Maisonneuve Ouest. Tel: (514) 985-2258. www. operademontreal.com*

Orchestre Métropolitain du Grand Montréal
For 25 years, the Orchestre Métropolitain du Grand Montréal has been performing at Place des Arts and touring the island of Montréal, presenting accessible programmes, multidisciplinary concerts, a talented young conductor and pre-performance conferences. *486 rue Sainte-Catherine Ouest. Tel: (514) 598-0870. www. orchestremetro politain.com*

Orchestre symphonique de Montréal
Québec's leading cultural ambassador treats audiences to some 100 concerts each year. Performances are held primarily at the Salle Wilfrid-Pelletier of Place des Arts, as well as in Old Montréal's Notre-Dame Basilica, but in warmer weather a series

of public concerts is featured in Montréal's parks.

286 boulevard de Maisonneuve Ouest.
Tel: (514) 842-9951.
www.osm.ca

Place des Arts

Featuring an impressive programme of music, theatre, dance, opera, song, comedy and musicals all year round, Place des Arts, located in the cultural heart of the city, is Canada's premiere entertainment centre. Its five halls total nearly 6,000 seats and its outdoor plaza plays host to the city's largest festivals. Guided backstage tours are also available.

260 boulevard de Maisonneuve Ouest.
Tel: (514) 842-2112.
www.pda.qc.ca

Saidye Bronfman Centre for the Arts

Québec's only multidisciplinary cultural institution, the Saidye Bronfman Centre for the Arts offers events and activities for all ages, including professional theatre, a School of Fine Arts, the Youth Institute and Art Gallery.

5170 rue de la Côte-Sainte-Catherine.
Tel: (514) 739-2301.
www.saidyebronfman.org

Théâtre du Nouveau Monde

The Théâtre du Nouveau Monde produces and presents major works from national and international repertoires while making room for exciting innovations. With well over 50 seasons, the TNM showcases plays of all origins where new forms speak directly to contemporary audiences.

84 rue Sainte-Catherine Ouest. Tel: (514) 866-8668. www.tnm.qc.ca

SPORTS STADIUMS/ ENTERTAINMENT VENUES

Atrium Le 1000

Located in the prestigious office building, Le 1000 de La Gauchetière, this indoor skating rink welcomes skaters all year round. Equipment rentals and snack counters available.

1000 rue de la Gauchetière Ouest.
Tel: (514) 395-0555.
www.le1000.com

Bell Centre/Montréal Canadiens Hockey Club

The home of the Montréal Canadiens Hockey Club, the Bell Centre was completed in 1996 and seats more than 21,000 sports enthusiasts. It is also a venue for rock concerts, classical music performances and family entertainment. Guided tours available.

1260 rue de la Gauchetière Street Ouest.
Tel: (514) 932-2582.
www.centrebell.ca

Hippodrome de Montréal

Horses and jockeys meet up at the Hippodrome de Montréal for exciting harness-racing action, on-track and inter-track. Features on-site video lottery terminals and a new-wave restaurant, Le Centaure. Group rates available.

7440 boulevard Décarie.
Tel: (514) 739-2741.
www.hdem.com

Québec City

ACCOMMODATION

Château Bonne Entente ★★–★★★★

Treat yourself to first-

lass accommodation
ith luxury spa and fine
ining in this little
uburb of Québec City.
400, chemin Sainte-Foy,
ainte-Foy.
el: (418) 653-522.
ww.
hateaubonneentente.com

airmont Le Château
rontenac ★★–★★★
he legendary Frontenac,
castle towering above
he cliffs of the St
awrence, is a 'must' for
hose new to Québec –
s well as for many
ho return.
 rue des Carrières.
el: (418) 692-3861.
mail: chateaufrontenac@
airomnt.com

Hôtel Manoir
Victoria ★–★★
The feel of a comfortable
friendly country inn
with complete 21st-
century amenities and
very friendly staff right
eside the cobblestone
streets of Vieux-Québec.
44 côte du Palais.
Tel: (418) 692-1030.
www.manoir-victoria.com

EATING OUT
Cochon Dingue ★
This 'little piggy'
restaurant is an
affordable and favourite

Québec City institution
specialising in huge
breakfast platters, steak
frites, pork spare ribs
(of course) and sinfully
rich desserts.
46 boulevard Champlain.
Tel: (418) 692-2013.
www.cochendingue.com

Crêperie le Petit
Château ★
Conveniently located
next to Le Château, this
favourite spot offers an
inexhaustible selection
of sweet and savoury
crepes, raclettes and
fondues.
5 rue Saint-Louis.
Tel: (418) 694-1616. www.
bonnesadressesvxqc.com

Le Vendôme ★★
A busy, bustling
atmosphere with aromas
of bouillabaisse, rack of
lamb and seafood dishes
created by an award-
winning chef.
36 côte de la Montagne.
Tel: (418) 692-0557. www.
restaurantvendome.com

Chez Rabalais ★★
At the very top of rue
Casse-cou ('Breakneck
stairs'), this small,
intimate dining room
blends a romantic glow
with excellent food in an
atmosphere of an

original 17th-century
Québec home.
2 rue Petit-Champlain.
Tel: (514) 694-9460.

Index

Acknowledgements

Thomas Cook wishes to thank the photographer DONALD NAUSBAUM, for the loan of the photographs reproduced in this book, to whom copyright in the photographs belongs (except the following):

BIGSTOCKPHOTO 12 (Cheever Calgary), 21 (Carvalho Boston); CASINORAMA 58; CHARLES DAWLEY 128; FLICKR.COM 5 (Boozysmurf); 14, 35 (Gary Wood); 50 (Roy Tanaka); 55 (Rick Harris); 56 (Vic Brincat); 59 (Gojumeister); 66 (Kim Scarborough); 86 (Grant); 88 (Philip Lai); 95 (William Klos); 101 (Kasia); 105 (Caroline Legrand); 129 (Bruce W Smith); 131 (Derek Hatfield); 140 (Ian Muttoo); 160 (Michelle Eriksson); FOTOLIA 4 (Benjamin Wahiche), 11 (Michael Pemberton), 83 (Doug Baines), 89 (Yaniv Nizard Lafrance); 127 (Gary Krevenky), 130 (Peter Goulah), 158 (Tammy McAllister); G FISCHER 125; HENRY PELHAM WINERY 45; HOCKLEY VALLEY RESORT 22, 23; PICTURES COLOUR LIBRARY 139; PIERRE LANGLOIS 109; QUEBEC TOURISM 97 (Yves Tessier, Tessima), 99 (J-F Bergeron/Enviro Foto); STRATFORD FESTIVAL OF CANADA 52 (Richard Bain); WIKIMEDIA COMMONS 67, 70 (Teresa Mitchell); WORLD PICTURES 37, 98, 102, 133, 145

Copy-editing: LYNN BRESLER for CAMBRIDGE PUBLISHING MANAGEMENT LTD

Index: KAROLIN THOMAS for CAMBRIDGE PUBLISHING MANAGEMENT LTD

Maps: PCGRAPHICS, Old Woking, UK

Proofreading: JAN McCANN for CAMBRIDGE PUBLISHING MANAGEMENT LTD

SEND YOUR THOUGHTS TO
BOOKS@THOMASCOOK.COM

We're committed to providing the very best up-to-date information in our travel guides and constantly strive to make them as useful as they can be. You can help us to improve future editions by letting us have your feedback. If you've made a wonderful discovery on your travels that we don't already feature, if you'd like to inform us about recent changes to anything that we do include, or if you simply want to let us know your thoughts about this guidebook and how we can make it even better – we'd love to hear from you.

Send us ideas, discoveries and recommendations today and then look out for your valuable input in the next edition of this title.

Emails to the above address, or letters to Travellers Project Editor, Thomas Cook Publishing, PO Box 227, Coningsby Road, Peterborough PE3 8SB, UK.

Please don't forget to let us know which title your feedback refers to!